REDEFINING SUCCESS

REDEFINING
SUCCESS

STORIES, SCIENCE, AND STRATEGIES
TO PRIORITIZE HAPPINESS AND
OVERCOME LIFE'S "OH SH!T" MOMENTS

MICHAEL BIARNES

NEW DEGREE PRESS

COPYRIGHT © 2021 MICHAEL BIARNES

All rights reserved.

REDEFINING SUCCESS

*Stories, Science, and Strategies to Prioritize Happiness
and Overcome Life's "Oh Sh!t" Moments*

ISBN   978-1-63730-806-6 *Paperback*

           978-1-63730-865-3 *Kindle Ebook*

           978-1-63730-982-7 *Ebook*

To my parents, Ramon and Maria, for making anything in life seem possible; to my sister, Marta, for always having my back; and to my wife, Steph, and dog, Zimmie, for putting up with my shenanigans every step of the way.

Contents

Introduction

——

Up until I was about ten years old, I dreamt about becoming a veterinarian. I wanted to help every kind of animal in the world. At that time, I even thought I'd be open to helping cats, and I am deathly allergic to cats![1] I could recite the most arbitrary facts about the most obscure animals on the planet—many thanks to Steve Irwin, "The Crocodile Hunter."

I had weekly magazines sent to my house, would watch every show possible, and would even look up animals in the encyclopedia. Yes, I'm aware that I just dated myself a bit with that example…But I vividly remember looking up the marmoset, an eight-inch-tall, adorable little monkey, in the good old encyclopedia to learn more about the fascinating miniature creature. At that stage in my life, being successful meant I would one day be helping animals. Period.

If only life could remain so simple, right?

---

[1] In hindsight that seems ridiculous because, let's be honest, the best compliment that can be given to a cat is that it "acts like a dog." So, I argue we should all just become dog people. But I know that's a losing argument, so to all you cat people out there, you do you! This book is also great for cat lovers.

Let's fast forward to my teenage years. At this stage of life, my definition for success changed drastically—presumably because I became more aware of pop culture, began idolizing athletes, and was exposed to new kinds of shows like *MTV Cribs*.[2]

If you asked me as a teenager, being successful meant you had some combination of power, fortune, and fame—preferably all three. Success came with a mansion, multiple sports cars, season tickets to your favorite sports teams (maybe even partial ownership), and the ability to travel the world. I envisioned having my own personal limo take me to my private jet which would, of course, fly me to my private island. Seems very private...perhaps too private?

Most of us wander through life striving to be successful. But have you ever stopped to think about what that really means? Chances are if you look back, "success" meant something wildly different depending on what stage of life you were in.

Let's return to our first case study—me, your MC, whose research throughout this book literally rips my teenage definition to shreds!

---

2   To my amazement, *MTV Cribs* is still on TV as of writing this book. In case you are unfamiliar, *MTV Cribs* is a show in which "reality stars, rappers, pro athletes, and more welcome cameras inside their souped-up spaces for exclusive tours." The show displays the most lavish lifestyles you can imagine, featuring the most ridiculous, opulent homes and over the top personalities (MTV, 2021).

While I'd like to think my definition for success matured as I grew older, I can't say that was the case until recently. After studying biology in undergrad, I spent my twenties cultivating my love of science to earn my master's in biotechnology and work my way up the ranks of the biopharma industry. I went from dreaming about helping animals to working in the field that performs animal testing...not exactly aligned with my ten-year-old version of success. But at least I was leveraging my love of science to try and improve patient outcomes, so I'll take it.

I was very focused on my salary and title at that stage in my life. There was a span in which I got four promotions in three years and it still wasn't enough for me to be happy. If you asked me, I could not get to the C-suite fast enough. Success was still very much tied to power, fortune, and fame.

If I'm being completely honest, I probably would still be pursuing that lifestyle and would not have Redefined Success for myself without the help of what I like to affectionately call an "Oh Shit Moment."

In case you're wondering, an "Oh Shit Moment" is an event that absolutely rocks your life and makes you question what the heck you're doing.

My "Oh Shit Moment" came in the form of my father's passing in 2018 after a two-year battle with cancer. That time in my late twenties absolutely crushed me! And while I don't wish for anyone to go through that kind of event, I will say my father's passing led to me undergoing a metamorphosis (animal reference—my love for animals lives on after all).[3]

While I would love to say that my "Oh Shit Moment" is unique and you will be spared from such events, in performing all of my research and interviews for this book, it's clear that these events, unfortunately, will touch everyone, even you, at various times in life.

So, after my father passed, I found myself asking:

- "Is this really what I want for my life?"
- "How do I balance all of the things that matter to me?"
- "Despite having what society deems to be 'success,' why do I still feel unhappy and unfulfilled?"

And it was with these thoughts that the seeds for this book were planted. It took a lot of soul-searching, deep reflection, researching, and honest conversations to recalibrate what mattered in life *to me*: to *Redefine Success*.

As I met people along this journey, I found one universal commonality among those people who I most looked up to; they, too, at some point in their lives, made a concerted effort to reflect and reprioritize the things that mattered most to them. Oftentimes these individuals would exchange what

---

3　I go into way more detail about my own personal journey leading up to my "Oh Shit Moment" and my path to Redefining Success in the conclusion! Go ahead and skip to that section if you're dying to hear more about me. I know, I know…you just want to hear about all of the awesome people I interviewed. I don't blame you at all, that's what I would want too!

others perceived to be "success" for something more important—their own personal definition of success.

But before we dive into their stories, we should establish some sort of baseline for what success actually means.

WHAT IS SUCCESS ANYWAY?

While 2020 brought about a lot of pain, sorrow, and grief due to the COVID-19 pandemic, it also forced many of us to look in the mirror and truly reflect on what matters most, something I feel is crucial in order to be truly successful. And while there is no wrong answer to the question "what matters most to you?" without taking a holistic view of your life and defining those truly important aspects for yourself, it is nearly impossible to feel fulfilled, happy, and satisfied, no matter how much perceived success you may attain.

All too often, we get caught up in our own lives, convincing ourselves we *need* that pay raise, new title, or promotion to be perceived as successful. We put on blinders and work our tails off to meet others' expectations and achieve specific goals. Meanwhile, life around us continues, and by the time we take a moment to pause and reflect, we realize the path we've been on all this time, may not have been the right path after all.

So, let's take a minute and try to define this ever-elusive concept of success. I would imagine most people lean toward Merriam-Webster's definition. After all, what better source for a definition than a dictionary? According to Merriam-Webster, success is:

- a "degree or measure of succeeding" (Not very helpful.)
- a "favorable or desired outcome" (A bit better?)
- "the attainment of wealth, favor, or eminence" (At least this gives some clarity!)

Admittedly, the first two leave a bit to be desired, but the third definition really tries to provide a definitive answer. It's scary how much this aligns with my teenage definition of success! The only problem is the definition is wrong.

If that third definition of success were true, lottery winners, social media influencers, and celebrities would all consider themselves to be successful, as they all achieved wealth, favor, or eminence, respectively. Yet, there are countless stories of lottery winners going bankrupt as they burn through cash in the pursuit of happiness. Despite this instant access to cash, lottery winners have a higher likelihood of declaring bankruptcy within three to five years than the average American (Hankins, 2011). Additionally, you can find endless examples of social media influencers and celebrities struggling with depression and searching for fulfillment. Unfortunately, these stories are in the media all too often.

So, what's the common factor among all of these examples? They may have achieved the dictionary definition of success, but they weren't happy or fulfilled. Shouldn't happiness and fulfillment at least be a part of the success equation? After all, if "success" does not bring happiness and fulfillment, what's the point? If we are not happy or fulfilled, we cannot consider ourselves to be successful. With this notion, it seems happiness and fulfillment *have* to be included in the definition.

So, what on earth does it actually mean to be successful?

Unfortunately, my answer may be massively disappointing, but I can't define success for you, because it's entirely personal. Fundamentally, success should be an internal metric, which is *defined by you.*

Admittedly, the journey to Redefining Success feels daunting because there is a seemingly endless number of factors to understand and consider before you are ready to truly determine that definition for yourself. But that's precisely what this book aims to help with! I promise you that if you put in the work, the fruits of Redefining Success are sweet and the juice is most definitely worth the squeeze.

OKAY, SO LET'S REDEFINE SUCCESS ALREADY!

In Part One, I'll introduce you to a number of wonderful and inspiring individuals who, regardless of wealth, title, or career trajectory, found themselves in dire need of change. Some had to experience something similar to what I went through, an "Oh Shit Moment," in which a sudden event made them seriously question what the hell they were doing with their lives. Others had a more gradual realization that something was off and change was needed, culminating with a brave decision to confront their own internal fears to make a drastic pivot.

From a former Olympian to individuals who climbed the corporate ladder just to leap from the top, to Hollywood producer turned fantasy football guru, to immigrant turned media icon, to college buddy turned BBQ expert—this book has something for everyone. Some examples are of individuals as ordinary as you and me while others are world-renowned superstars.

Regardless of social status, wealth, or career accomplishments, the one truth I have found in all of my interviews and research is that at some point in life, everyone found themselves asking some version of "is this really what I want in life?"

The folks I met with were extraordinary enough to do something about it when their answer ultimately wound up being "no." Whether that meant modifying goals and aspects of their lives related to their career, family, finances, health, personal interests, community, relationships, or some combination, this book will share tactics of how these bold souls Redefined Success for themselves.

In Part Two, I'll synthesize and share the science, mentalities, frameworks, and strategies I uncovered throughout this journey so you can ultimately define success for yourself! I also include exercises, resources, and workbook pages for you along the way so you can implement the aspects that resonate most into your own life.

By the end, you will craft your own definition for success. On the way, I hope some of the stories I share will inspire you or at the very least make you chuckle and even reflect a bit. Hopefully, some of the questions, tools, and research I pose will help you distill your own definition by encouraging you to consider what really matters to you. Because without an understanding of what you truly care about, happiness and fulfillment will remain elusive, no matter how much you achieve.

However, by creating your own definition, you can align your life accordingly. I'm no guru (far from it), but through sharing the stories of extraordinary individuals, my personal journey, and some fascinating research, my hope is to give you a "cheat code" to Redefine Success for yourself. Ultimately, it will be your own answers and actions that enable you to attain true *success*.

PART 1

STORIES & RESEARCH

CHAPTER 1

Without Happiness, What's the Point?

Happiness Should Be Included in Every Definition of Success

If you ask my wife, I have a problem: an addiction to fantasy sports. I started playing fantasy baseball and fantasy football when I was fourteen years old. Today, I play almost every fantasy sport you can think of.

There are literally two days a year my wife looks forward to just because there is no stressing to be had about my fantasy sports lineups: the two days surrounding the MLB all-star game. These are the only two days of the year when there isn't a single sporting event scheduled for any of my beloved fantasy leagues. That's right...363 days of fantasy sports a year.

Saying it out loud really does make it seem like I have a problem. Thankfully, my wife is awesome and puts up with my quirkiness!

Despite loving all of the fantasy sports I play, nothing beats fantasy football season for me. Each year, my friends and I get together to catch up and relive our college days (albeit nowadays the hangovers are *far* worse than they used to be), all in the name of fantasy football.[4]

Every year, without fail, I listen to each episode of ESPN's *Fantasy Focus Football* podcast featuring Matthew Berry, Field Yates, and Stephania Bell. I also avidly follow just about every TV show, article, app, and blog attached to Matthew Berry. During football season, Matthew is basically an honorary roommate in our household. And yes, that does sound a bit creepy now as I write it, but we already established I have a problem.

Let me explain a bit further. Matthew Berry is *the* fantasy football guy at ESPN (I would argue in the entire industry). Through his work in what he likes to call "fake football," he has won an Emmy Award, is a *New York Times* best-selling author for his book *Fantasy Life*, has been inducted into the Fantasy Sports Trade Association Hall of Fame and Fantasy Sports Writers Association Hall of Fame, has been awarded seven podcasting awards, and produces content that routinely ranks among the most trafficked stories on all of ESPN for the entire year (ESPN Press Room, 2021).

---

4   I am the commissioner of The PSU (Penn State University) Fantasy Football League with my college buddies, which has been going on since 2009. That's twelve years and counting as of the writing of this book! I just so happen to have been champion in four of those twelve years. I had to throw this fun fact in to annoy my leaguemates.

You see, Matthew Berry has a way of making fantasy football *fun*. He is likeable, funny, and knowledgeable without coming across as snobby. Despite all of the statistics that are part of fantasy football, he makes the game accessible, so much so that my wife even enjoys listening to the podcast from time to time.

He and his team have won so many podcasting awards that they had to be deemed a "legacy podcast" so other podcasts in the category could have a chance to win.

At this point, you probably get it. But if I say, "fantasy football," you should say "Matthew Berry."

So naturally, when I started writing this book, I thought to myself, "This is my chance! Matthew has a fantastic story about chasing happiness to achieve all he has accomplished. I have to reach out." So, I drafted an email and sent it to Matthew, never expecting to hear from him. The man has over one million Twitter followers and is the face of fantasy football; there's no way he would respond.

Of course, less than a week after sending my email, I got a response—"Sure"—with the contact information to set up the call.

Now, I won't lie, I was fanboying harder than you could even imagine when I saw that email come through. Go ahead, picture me going crazy. Whatever you're picturing is probably not extreme enough. Of course, my in-laws were in town when I got the email so they got to witness my embarrassing display.

In my conversation with Matthew, I learned that while he enjoyed fantasy football as a passion from the time he was fourteen years old (hey, that's the same age I started!), he had other dreams for himself professionally.

After graduating from Syracuse in 1992, Matthew aspired to enter the realm of Hollywood. He worked his tail off and eventually landed himself a production assistant role on *The George Carlin Show*. Yes, one of Matthew's first jobs was working with the amazingly funny George Carlin. And while Matthew admits it was a ton of work, from all of his accounts, George Carlin was supremely gracious with his time and treated everyone with respect and compassion.

I am simply speculating, but I imagine this kindness from a bigtime star helped mold Matthew into the gracious and considerate celebrity he is today. Why else would he take a call with me?

Matthew spent the next twelve years "scratching and clawing" his way into the screenwriting industry, eventually writing for the hit sitcom *Married...with Children* starring Ed O'Neill as Al Bundy and the classic movie sequel *Crocodile Dundee in Los Angeles*. He even found a way to parlay his Hollywood accomplishments into a side hustle writing about his passion—fantasy football.

It turned out the owners of *Rotoworld*, a fantasy football blog, were huge Al Bundy fans, so they let Matthew write articles for their website—something he did for free, mind you. From this experience, he eventually started his very own fantasy football sites on the side.

By all accounts, Matthew had made his Hollywood dream a reality! And yet, despite it all, it was not what he had hoped for.

During an interview on David Meltzer's podcast, *The Playbook*, in 2020, Matthew shared, "I was incredibly depressed, like massively depressed, like I hated my life. And I couldn't understand it because I had this high-paying job as a screenwriter, I was married, I had my health, I had friends, and I couldn't figure it out."

Matthew's confusion was not unfounded. On paper, he had all of the things we are told to work toward in life to be considered "successful," yet he was incredibly unhappy. Unfortunately, many of us face the same feelings even when life is seemingly going well. This begs the question—we know what happiness feels like, but what is it really?

Happiness is such a ubiquitous term, apparently easy to identify yet it can feel difficult to attain and nearly impossible to maintain.

It turns out the definition of happiness can be traced back all the way to everyone's favorite ancient Greek philosopher: Aristotle.[5] Aristotle reasoned there were two components to happiness: hedonia (pleasure) and eudaimonia (life well-lived, fulfillment, meaning, or satisfaction) (Kringelbach and

---

5   I can feel Socrates and Plato cursing at me as I write that line. Plato taught Aristotle for crying out loud! Regardless of who your favorite Greek philosopher is, the fact we still cite him today is pretty remarkable. Aristotle lived from 384–322 BCE and we still reference his work over twenty-three hundred years later—talk about a legacy!

Berridge, 2010). To this day, positive psychologists continue to think of happiness in this construct.

Hedonia is associated with doing the things that feel good and bring you pleasure. These are often shorter-term bursts of contentment like eating a delicious donut, treating yourself to a spa day, or taking some time to go fishing. All wonderful things, but unfortunately, it is only one part of the happiness equation.

Eudaimonia, on the other hand, is typically longer-term and is how we derive meaning and virtue in our lives. Examples of eudaimonia include raising a child and seeing them flourish, completing a long-term goal like writing a book (hey, that's me!), living up to your own personal principles and ideals, providing mentorship to others, or taking care of someone you love. Eudaimonia helps to give purpose and meaning to your life—something we all yearn for.

Can you identify things that bring you hedonia (pleasure) and eudaimonia (fulfillment) in your life? Take a moment to reflect and identify a few aspects that bring you pleasure and fulfillment in your life today. Can you think of anything that would increase your pleasure or fulfillment? If you're struggling with coming up with a list, no worries! We'll have plenty of exercises in subsequent chapters to work through this together.

In a 2020 episode of *Clear+Vivid with Alan Alda*, Yale professor and positive psychologist Dr. Laurie Santos elaborated on how psychologists today think about happiness: "Social scientists tend to think of happiness in two parts. One is how happy you are with your life and [the other being] how happy you are in your life. So how happy you are with your life is what researchers call life satisfaction...How do you think your life is going? How satisfied are you with your life?...But there's also how happy you are in your life. Are you experiencing lots of positive emotions? Do you have relatively limited negative emotions you can handle?...If you're... really satisfied with your life and day to day, you have a lot of laughter, joy, and positivity and not as much anger and sadness, then I can say for the most part you're happy."

It doesn't sound like much has changed since our friend Aristotle pondered about happiness back in Athens.

To add a bit more context, being happy doesn't mean you never feel sad, angry, discontent, frustrated, etc. Unfortunately, those negative emotions will rock you from time to time no matter what.

That said, those individuals who are truly happy routinely feel more positive feelings than negative feelings and also feel satisfied in the life they are living. When negative emotions do pop up, happy individuals are better prepared to deal with them in a healthy way because they generally have a sense of optimism things will improve (Cherry and Goldman, 2020).

Armed with this new information regarding happiness, let's return to Matthew's conflict and see how he overcame his feelings of depression despite his "success."

Finally, in 2004, after some help from therapy and countless hours of reflection, Matthew vividly remembers thinking, "I gotta get out. I gotta get out." As he pondered his next steps, Matthew came to realize the silly, free articles he had been writing about fantasy football were what brought him the most joy in his life.

When thinking about what kept him up at night and got him out of bed in the morning, Matthew responded, "[The] things I thought about were the websites. Not the movie studios, the big-time producers, the movie stars, the big pitch we had coming up, or...the problem we were having with a particular scene—none of those things that were paying the bills; just these dumb little websites I was trying to make a go of."

So that's precisely what he decided to focus his efforts on. "I know it sounds crazy that I've got this kind of exciting, glamorous Hollywood writer/producer job and I'm making good money and I want to give it all up to try to make a living at fake football. But yeah, that's what I wanted to do. It seems obvious now, but at that point in 2004, fantasy football wasn't what it is today...It was considered very niche, very nerdy. It was only online. And at that point, online wasn't what it is today. Writing digital [content] wasn't a way to make a living."

To put this more in perspective, when Matthew decided to plunge headfirst into the deep end of the fantasy sports pool, there were about 13.5 million total fantasy sports players in North America (Sports Management Degree Hub, 2021). People were not spending much money in the industry because the barriers to entry (mainly technology) were still high. Daily fantasy sports had not been invented yet, so fantasy sports were only for those who were truly dedicated for a full season of fun.

Fast-forward to today, where daily fantasy sports, smart-phones, and I argue individuals like Matthew Berry have more than quadrupled the number of people who participate in fantasy sports up to sixty million people in North America (Willingham, 2020). In 2019, the industry had grown to become an 18.6 billion dollar industry with estimates that the industry will continue to explode, reaching 48.6 billion dollars by 2027 (Valuates Reports, 2020). These are absolutely staggering numbers that could not have been predicted back in 2004.

But enough about the booming fantasy sports industry. Refocusing our attention on Matthew's bold decision, what's more striking to me is that Matthew realized this major life change would require a three-step process.

1. Understand and admit he was unhappy. (Check!)
2. Reflect and have the realization of what needs to change and how to make that change (i.e., he wanted to quit showbiz for fantasy sports writing—so far so good!)
3. Have the guts to make the change and tell his loved ones about the life pivot. (That sounds a bit more daunting!)

This third step was supremely challenging as it meant not only coming to terms with changing something that had become part of his identity after dedicating twelve years of his life to it, but also having the courage to tell his family, friends, and colleagues his plan.

Matthew remembers having conversations with his brother and parents explaining, "This is what's gonna make me happy. I want to chase happiness. I no longer want to chase money. I no longer want to chase fame or success. I really just want to chase happiness. And once I said that out loud, people were like, 'Good, go for you.'"

While this step of telling friends and family weighs heavily on most of us who are pondering a change, I'm happy to report that every single one of the incredible people I interviewed for this book received a similar reaction to Matthew. There was some initial questioning from loved ones to ensure they were truly headed down a good path, but that was quickly followed by a heaping pile of love and support from their network, leading them to feel simultaneously overwhelmed, surprised, and relieved. While merely anecdotal, it is supremely reassuring and comforting to know that in times of change, those whom we cherish most will help propel us forward to achieve our dreams.

So, Matthew wrote one more script for Hollywood to create more of a financial cushion for himself and then transitioned away from his lavish life as a writer/producer to slumming it as a fantasy sports blogger.[6]

To really put the transition into perspective, Matthew shared, "I was making one hundred bucks a week at Rotoworld. I wrote for free for the first year and a half, then I think they

---

6   This idea of creating a financial cushion for yourself before making a career pivot in the pursuit of happiness is a great way to help to de-risk the transition. If your next gig comes with a higher income, then, to quote the great Ron Swanson from *Parks and Recreation*, "bully for you." But for those who are considering a pay cut to better align your career with your priorities, strategically planning ahead by taking some time to save will greatly increase your probabilities of achieving your desired lifestyle without having to make drastic cuts at a later time.

started to pay me like twenty-five bucks a column. I think I eventually worked my way up to fifty bucks a column or something like that. If they'd said, 'We can't pay you anymore,' I would have still done it for free because I loved it."

Matthew took on the challenge and used the same energy and dedication he leveraged to enter the ultracompetitive TV and film industry to growing his fantasy football side hustle into a full-blown profession. To paraphrase legendary singer-song writer Jimmy Buffett, one of Matthew's favorite musicians, his path required luck, hard work, and a little bit of talent.[7]

"I started my own blog but I realized I wasn't going to be able to buy any advertising, so the best way for me to promote the website was me. So just hustle. I went to every radio station, every website, and every TV station I could find saying, 'I'll write for you for free. I'll come on your air for free. Just mention my website, just link back to my website, just send me the traffic.'"[8]

With all of this hustle, Matthew's personal brand and fantasy football prowess grew—so much so that in 2007, ESPN bought his website and offered Matthew a fulltime job. Matthew joined the massive conglomerate and never looked back, using ESPN's unrivaled platform to help grow the fantasy sports industry to the heights we see today. But in reflecting,

---

7 Jimmy Buffett's fans are affectionately known as Parrot Heads. Matthew Berry is a Parrot Head!

8 Funny enough, one of Matthew's favorite expressions to say ironically on his podcast is "nothing good comes from hustling." At one point, you could even buy a T-shirt from his personal website that said that!

Matthew sees that as his own personal voyage to happiness and, ultimately, success.

"It literally was about saving my life and just wanting to chase happiness and my passion. What's crazy is that by doing that, by leaving show business and chasing happiness, I went from behind the scenes to onscreen. I've now been on TV. I've won an Emmy. I've been in movies. I have a role in *Avengers: Endgame*. I had to leave Hollywood to get into a movie. I had to leave Hollywood to be on TV. And I've had so much more success, financial and otherwise, by just chasing happiness and not worrying about anything else."

My honorary roommate's decision to chase happiness has led to a remarkable list of accomplishments and an inspiring improvement in his own definition of success. He left his swanky Hollywood lifestyle, which society often idolizes, for a more austere and uncertain path surrounding a silly little game that has blossomed into a behemoth of an industry.

Through careful assessment of what mattered most to him, he was able to carefully plan and de-risk his decision for a career pivot. And while happiness was his goal, the accolades and financial rewards that followed were a nice cherry on top. Didn't I tell you it was a hell of a story?

Does this interview and incredible story justify my unhealthy, 363-day addiction to fantasy sports? Perhaps not. But since it's bringing me hedonia, I say it's a win!

KEY CHAPTER TAKEAWAYS

- Just because you attain or achieve what society deems to be success (job, spouse, wealth, friends, etc.), doesn't mean it will lead to happiness. Living a life aligned with your own personal priorities is crucial in our quest for happiness.

- When trying to determine what motivates you, ask yourself: What keeps me up at night? What gets me out of bed in the morning?

- After defining your priorities and what you want, hustle, hustle, and hustle some more to align your life around your priorities.

- If you are considering a pivot, through careful planning and thoughtful execution, you can de-risk the upcoming change in your life.

- Despite the nerves you may feel about opening up to friends and family about your thoughts and feelings, remember they will likely be supportive and ultimately want to see you be happy.

- Happiness incorporates both pleasure and fulfillment. Without satisfying both pieces of the equation, happiness will remain fleeting.

CHAPTER 2

There's More than Meets the Eye

Even People Who Appear to Have Life All
Figured Out Struggle to Redefine Success

Take a second to think about a friend that you feel has figured out the game of life.

What I mean by that is they seemingly have always known what they wanted to do from day one, they have their priorities in order, they have amazing life stories, they have one thousand friends (no, not Facebook friends or Twitter connections—legitimate friends), and they almost always seem happy.

Let's be honest, while you feel blessed to have this person in your life because they're absolutely amazing, you also envy the ridiculous awesomeness that is their life.

For me, this person is Mike O'Donnell. Mike and I went to high school together but really got close during our time at Penn State. We wound up being college roommates and became way too adept at pranking one another. For instance, Mike loved to "booby trap" the room so objects would fall on my head whenever I opened the door. Yes, we are fully aware we are ridiculous.

Mike has been a close friend for over ten years now and was even one of the groomsmen at my wedding. He also happens to be one of the ten members of my college fantasy football league I mentioned in Chapter One.[9]

Because of the league, every year, we get together for mayhem and debauchery during the draft. Or at least we should get together. Over the years, Mike has dialed in to our drafts from Montreal, Lithuania, and Italy because of his worldly escapades. I told you, his life is incredible!

So, if you would have asked me before I interviewed Mike for this book, I would have shared Mike knew what he wanted for his life since day one. He was a born entrepreneur.

Since college, he has built a thriving business around grilling equipment called Cave Tools. He has leveraged Cave Tools to travel the world. Mike was supposed to be my example of someone who figured life out and could share sage advice of how to Redefine Success for yourself when you're young.

---

9 To borrow a phrase from Matthew Berry, I crush him like a grape every single year! Mike only has two championships compared to my four—how embarrassing.

After a bit of catching up, I started our interview together with, "So I wanted to interview you to learn about how you figured out what you wanted in life at such an early age. Help my readers understand how you avoided an 'Oh Shit Moment' but still found what you wanted."

Mike retorted, "Yeah, it's interesting. From people outside looking in, the idea is I always knew what I wanted to do, but I don't feel that way. I guess it certainly looks that way." Let this be a lesson; no matter how much you plan ahead, no interview goes as expected. So, naturally, I needed to go down the rabbit hole that metaphorically appeared before me to learn more.

In college, Mike decided against a traditional business internship with a Fortune 500 company to work an unpaid internship he felt would provide him greater opportunities to learn and grow. When describing this internship, all I know is it was with his friend, Justin. Notice this does not have the same ring to it as interning with Procter & Gamble or Coca-Cola?

But Mike is the poster child for the growth mindset—something we will explore at length in Chapter Ten. Essentially, if Mike feels he has an opportunity to learn or gain experience, he will say yes to that opportunity, even if it means giving up something that may provide greater incentives in the short term. I believe this character trait is largely responsible for all he has accomplished to date.

In college, he attempted to build two businesses, but they did not grow as he had hoped. So, with a mountain of student loans to pay off, Mike did the responsible thing by getting a day job selling fire alarm and sprinkler inspection contracts.

And boy, oh boy, did he hate it! "I got into this rut where I would go to work, hate my job, come home, watch TV for like four or five hours, go to bed, wake up, and do it again. I just hated everything."

Welcome to Mike's wakeup call—his "Oh Shit Moment."

At that point in his life, Mike was journaling and meditating daily to help elucidate some of his thoughts and feelings. He also spoke with his now mentor, Justin (remember him?), who convinced him living with this hatred and unhappiness was no way to live at all.

Justin suggested Mike attend a conference in Houston on search engine optimization (SEO) to better understand the business and career opportunities in the space. Despite knowing no one at the conference and very little about SEO, Mike saw an opportunity to learn (growth mindset again) and booked his ticket for Houston.

Mike, being the social butterfly he is, hit it off with another Philly sports fan who was in the process of building his own entrepreneurial venture and needed help growing his business in Montreal. That turned into a job opportunity, which ultimately led to Mike attending one of our fantasy football drafts from Montreal.

This unlikely partnership flourished and eventually led to Mike being offered a whopping 40 percent of the company because of the massive growth the business had experienced since he had joined as an employee—all of this from randomly meeting a guy at a conference and both being Philly sports fans! But to this too-good-to-be-true equity offer, Mike said, "No, thanks."

"I ended up turning it down. And everybody, including my parents, responded with 'What the f*%#?'"

He rationalized, "I'm twenty-two. This is an amazing deal, but it's only 40 percent. While that's great for me now, in a couple years, this is going to eat up inside me. All it is is a job with equity. And even though it's amazing now, I think the right move longer-term is to break out back on my own."

Talk about chutzpah and self-confidence!

From that point on, Mike attempted a few more ventures that didn't quite pan out as he had hoped. These ventures were not in vain, though, as through each failure, Mike learned valuable lessons he could apply in the future, including mistakes to avoid, opportunities to grasp, and efficiencies to employ. Another valuable and often overlooked trait of any "success" story is embracing failure and learning from it—again, the growth mindset in action.

Though he had to make sacrifices in his personal life to afford this entrepreneurial lifestyle, the happiness and fulfillment Mike felt brought him new life!

Finally, Mike found his sweet spot with grilling equipment. Of course, you like to think every company that thrives is steeped in research and supremely well-thought out, but think again.

Mike took a training course about how to sell products on Amazon. After doing a bit of research, he figured out his business plan was fairly product agnostic, meaning that his business strategy could work across a number of different product types. "I came down to five products in my market research: tealight candles, whiteboards, elongated toilet seats, birdhouses, and grill brushes. It was the middle of summer, when grill brushes sell really well. So, I did grill brushes. Cave Tools was going to be a man brand. It was anything man cave, just a man brand. But being the amazing marketer I was, I totally forgot about seasonality and the fact nobody buys grill brushes in winter." You've got to love the honesty!

Despite the seasonality effect, that first year, Mike effectively broke even—but to him, it was like winning a marathon! "That was a success…I just learned! I'd never even shipped a package to a friend before at the UPS Store." Seriously, Mike? I sometimes question how he has survived this long.

He continued, "I learned how to manufacture something, create a brand, import, pay import duties and fees…I got to do everything I could in marketing and business…For me, that was a giant success. I don't give a shit that I made no money." Again, you've got to love the honesty and growth mindset!

It's important to note that throughout the early years of his journey, Mike leaned on his family, friends, and network to help him to pursue his dream responsibly. While he could have taken a more traditional job at any time, he understood the tradeoffs and forged ahead with building his company and desired lifestyle.

Mike continued to grow Cave Tools and leverage his growth mindset to network, join entrepreneurship communities, and travel the world. Despite all of his work to build Cave Tools, he always maintained "there's so much more to life than just work. I look forward to spending a lot more time on other areas of life."

In 2014, Mike flew to Lithuania to attend Sovereign Academy, a five-day intensive business and financial boot camp focused on entrepreneurship, mentorship, and networking. Admittedly, that was a bit on a whim, but it opened a plethora of doors and introduced him to a tremendous network of individuals. He remembers telling his family about this and having one family member ask, "Where the hell is Lithuania?"

Mike responded, "I don't know, there's the little three fingers at the top of the map." (Yes, he was talking about Finland, Norway, and Sweden.) Mike admits he had no idea where it was on a map.

While I laughed *a lot* at Mike at that point of the interview, I must admit that I could not pinpoint Lithuania on a map either.[10] But as he reflected on that trip, he acknowledged, "That was scary shit. I had never traveled alone anywhere."

---

10   For reference, Lithuania touches the Baltic Sea in northern Europe. It's located south of Latvia, northwest of Belarus, and northeast of Poland and Kaliningrad.

That said, he attributes much of his success to finding groups of likeminded entrepreneurs (like this one in Lithuania) who could empathize with his entrepreneurial lifestyle. Mike joined entrepreneurship-focused networking groups like Sovereign Man, Maverick1000 (founded by Yanik Silver— we will meet him in Chapter Five), and the DC (short for Dynamite Circle).

Mike's mindset led to a nontraditional, albeit more exciting, lifestyle that included the rollercoaster of owning a small business, traveling the world, and not settling down in one location for too long. He found he often needed to answer questions from friends and family about his future and non-traditional way of life. But Mike had it clear in his head: "At some point, I have to live my life. I can't just live other people's lives...Freedom is very important to me. I care about it most."

Living your life aligned with your priorities is exactly what this book is about! It sounds like Mike has Redefined Success for himself after all.

Now in his thirties, Mike finds his priorities are changing, admitting he finds himself more focused on family, establishing some roots, and building deeper connections. Like many of the examples in this book, Mike's North Star appears to be shifting and a life pivot is in the works. But unlike earlier in his life, Mike is proactively defining what he wants and realigning his life around his new priorities.

True to his brand, Mike has remained incredibly reflective. He has the uncanny ability to be thoughtful about what he prioritizes and how to design his life so it aligns with his priorities. In my opinion, that is the true hallmark of success. What does that mean for Mike in the next few years? I'm not sure he knows yet, but consider me excited to see what Mike decides to do next!

KEY CHAPTER TAKEAWAYS

- There is always more than meets the eye! No matter what you may think or how others may present themselves, everyone has their own challenges and struggles in life.
- Identifying what is important to you is crucial in Redefining Success for yourself. Only after you have defined your priorities can you begin to live better aligned with them.
- Embracing the growth mindset is crucial in our personal development to enable honest reflection, learning, and progress. There is more on this in Chapter Ten.
- Embracing failure and learning from it is essential to your growth. After a failure, be sure to reflect on what worked well, what lessons you learned, and opportunities you have for improvement.
- The best decision may not come with immediate rewards. Think thoughtfully about what you want and make your decisions based upon your priorities.
- Sometimes in life, the key is simply to say "yes" to the opportunities that present themselves. Mike showed this time and time again, refusing to let good get in the way of great. Despite how enjoyable it is to sit on a couch, nothing in life changes by sitting in your living room. As they say, "If nothing changes, nothing changes."

CHAPTER 3

Goal Achievement, FOMO, and the Desire for More

Goal Achievement Alone Won't Yield the Happiness & Fulfillment You Seek

"I'll be happy when _____ ." Go ahead, take a minute and fill out the blank.

We all have these thoughts from time to time. We convince ourselves if only we could find that perfect relationship, get that dream job, or purchase that brand-new house with a white picket fence, then we would finally be at peace and enjoy each and every day.

Terry McDougall was no different. In an interview, she shared with me, "Many of us who are high achievers have chased that North Star throughout our whole lives. We've been taught to do that and we've been rewarded for doing that. When I was younger, I wanted to become a chief marketing officer (CMO). That was my goal."

And did she ever work her butt off to get there—over thirty years of corporate business experience in various financial services firms with countless promotions along the way. She even earned her MBA to put the cherry on top of her resume.

Finally, she got what she had been dreaming of—the "white glove treatment" during an interview to become CMO of a major division of a bigtime national bank. Of course, she crushed the interview and got the job offer. All the prestige, power, money, and perks she had been working tirelessly for decades to achieve had finally come to fruition!

As Terry reflected on that momentous achievement during our interview together, the next words that came out were: "Yeah, I didn't f*%#ing want to do it...my feelings about the offer were visceral."

With all of the proper interview etiquette in the world, naturally my mouth dropped to the floor in dismay.

It turns out this unexpected feeling of unhappiness despite reaching our goals is quite common and perfectly natural due to something happiness experts call "hedonic adaptation," the ability to acclimate ourselves to our changing environments to ensure no matter how good or bad our circumstances become, our happiness levels never over-cal-ibrate for too long (Evans, 2019).[11]

While it may seem cruel, this piece of human evolution is vitally important for those truly tough times in our lives: the death of a loved one, major injury, financial ruin, get-ting fired, etc. Hedonic adaptation allows us to power on and slowly improve until, one day, we feel like ourselves again.

Unfortunately, this also means when we achieve something great, such as a new job, great relationship, or fancy new car, the amazing happiness and fulfillment we feel also dissipate over time. Welp, that's disheartening. Good thing for hedonic adaptation; I'll feel better in no time!

In fact, Dr. Gillian Mandich, founder of The International Happiness Institute of Health Science Research, takes it a step further. Dr. Mandich asserts that the belief you will be happy once you achieve your goals is not only erroneous due to hedonic adaptation, but also a toxic mindset that can lead to a flurry of negative emotions and even depression (Evans, 2019).

One of the leading experts in the field, Dr. Laurie Santos, professor of psychology at Yale University with a PhD from Harvard, has spent years researching the human mind, hap-piness, and positive psychology. Dr. Santos has seen firsthand

---

11   Happiness experts are a thing? Apparently so. These individuals focus on positive psychology and dedicate their lives to researching what makes individuals thrive.

the toxicity that can come from expecting happiness after goal completion.[12]

In a 2020 interview on *Clear+Vivid with Alan Alda,* Dr. Santos shared she witnesses a similar phenomenon with her students. "When I took on the role, I thought, 'College students [are] super happy.' I thought back to my college days and thought I was just going to see students who were partying and happy. [But in actuality], when I took on the new role, I saw incredible mental health dysfunction. It was kind of shocking [to see] the level of students who were depressed, anxious, or just so stressed it was hard for them to function... [At] first, I got really worried, [thinking], 'What is wrong with Yale or what is wrong with the Ivy League schools?'... But then, as I dug into the data, I realized this was not just Yale students."

In a recent national survey, she explained 40 percent of college students reported being too depressed to function most days, 60 percent shared they felt overwhelmingly anxious, and over 10 percent said they had recently thought about suicide. This feeling for students starts almost immediately after getting their acceptance letter. Despite winning the "college lottery" as she calls it, many of these newly accepted students report feeling a "moment of deep despair" after the immediate elation dissipates.

---

12   Dr. Santos' passion for this line of research dates back to when she accepted a new role at Yale as the head of Silliman College, something she compares to being the head of the Gryffindor House in the Hogwarts School of Witchcraft and Wizardry in *Harry Potter.* Shout-out to all the *Harry Potter* fans!

This feeling of unhappiness is not only common among undergraduates, but also for graduate students and working professionals.

In an interview with venture capitalist Patrick McGinnis, he shared his memories of feeling this anxiety upon arriving at Harvard Business School (HBS) to pursue his Master of Business Administration (MBA).

"Inside of an MBA environment, you have a million classes, jobs, trips, and all the stuff that typically happens when you're in an MBA program. I just tried to do it all to the point where I was constantly feeling a sense of anxiety and stress, which I named FOMO, short for 'fear of missing out.' I even wrote an article in a school newspaper back in 2004 called, "Social Theory at HBS: McGinnis' Two FOs.""

I know what you're thinking: "There's no way Patrick *invented* the term 'FOMO'." Go ahead, google the origins of "FOMO."

I kid you not; Patrick is actually credited with the creation of this now ubiquitous term! In case you're wondering, the other less commonly used "FO" Patrick coined is "FOBO," fear of a better option. FOBO is often the culprit for the feeling of FOMO.

As Patrick neared the end of his MBA and considered his next steps, he felt he had to return to the world of private equity. "So much of my identity was tied up in private equity and all my friends were in private equity." Now, you might think to yourself, "Wow, if a profession is so intertwined with Patrick's identity, Patrick must really be passionate about it."

Not so much. Patrick picked up private equity from an unlikely source and simply continued with it long enough that it grew on him like a fungus. We'll need to go back in time for this part of our story; bear with me.

This origin story takes us back to Patrick's days at Georgetown University, where he was pursuing his bachelor's degree. Like most ambitious and eager undergraduates, Patrick was trying to figure out what he wanted to be when he grew up. Let's be honest, most of us are still trying to figure that out, no matter how old we get.

Patrick had considered being a trade negotiator or working in the public sector, but after doing some research, he decided he wanted more glitz and prestige in his life. One day, Patrick found his career inspiration in a rather unusual place.

Patrick shared, "I remember this so well actually. I read an article in a magazine...about a kid who was right out of college and made 75,000 dollars a year, which at that time was a ton of money, and he was drinking champagne out of a limo in Argentina on his business trip. I just wanted that for myself. The money and the glamour really appealed to me even though I had no idea what investment bankers did. So that got me to apply to all these investment banks."

So, fresh out of college, Patrick landed himself an investment banking job, which he confessed he hated. But at least it allowed him to live a similar life style to his magazine idol.

After a short stint in investment banking, he switched over to the private equity and venture capital arm of the same company, a role which he admittedly "liked enough," but continued for a few years, nonetheless. With a few years of private equity experience under his belt and now firmly part of his identity, Patrick decided to pursue his fulltime MBA at the prestigious Harvard Business School. And so, we are all caught up!

As Patrick continued his post-MBA job search in hopes of reentering the lucrative private equity industry, he found it difficult and, unfortunately, he only received one offer, which he begrudgingly accepted.

"I got one job, which was at a small PE (private equity) fund based in New Jersey…and I signed the offer letter and I knew I was gonna hate it. But it was the only thing I had and I wanted to have the security of having a job. It was like living inside of *Office Space*, except I didn't have anyone to hang out with.[13] I was alone. And so, I was there for three months. On the third month anniversary, I took a nap under my desk and I woke up from that nap and thought, 'I need to get the heck out of here. This place is killing me.'"

And so, in 2005, Patrick found another job, except this time it was with a major player in the private equity space: American International Group (AIG). Yes, the very same AIG that could be found in nearly every headline during the 2008 financial crisis due to its—to put it nicely—*questionable*

---

13 *Office Space* is a hilarious 1999 film about three friends who hate their jobs and come up with an elaborate scheme to rebel against the company and their greedy boss. The movie has a star-studded cast, includes hypnosis, and has iconic scenes about destroying an office printer. Also, don't mess with Milton's stapler (IMDb, 2021)!

practices. Between 2008 and 2009, AIG's stock lost a striking 97 percent of its value and needed to be bailed out.

That time was absolutely devastating for the employees at AIG, including Patrick, who found himself so stressed, miserable, and unhealthy from the toll of this experience he was eventually put on a heart monitor!

As Patrick reflected on that time of his life, he remembered thinking to himself, "Even before AIG blew up, I worked really hard...and I achieved more and made more money in the previous year than I ever thought I would when I was younger, and yet, I'm completely miserable. What's wrong with this picture?"

How can this be? How can it be that Terry was finally offered her dream role as a CMO, Dr. Santos' students had just made it into Yale, and Patrick earned more money than he ever dreamed of, and yet, they were all tragically unhappy?

Well, it turns out our intuitions about happiness are wrong.

Instead of thinking about happiness as a destination (i.e., getting into an Ivy League school or getting a dream job), we should be thinking about it more as a mindset, a collection of behaviors, and an appreciation of the journey.

When asked about achieving happiness in her 2020 appearance on *Clear+Vivid with Alan Alda*, Dr. Santos explained, "We think what we need to do is to change our circumstances. [I] have to switch my job, or get a new partner, or just change something big about my life. [But in reality, this only works]

if you're in pretty dire circumstances, like if you're in a ref-
ugee camp [or] if you don't have enough money to put food
on your table."

There is a plethora of research that shows that if you have a roof
over your head, can put food on the table, have access to healthcare, and have even a bit of disposable income, changing your
circumstances won't affect your happiness the way you think.

Believe it or not, a global study performed by Dr. Andrew Jebb
at Purdue University in 2018 found the income that brought
the highest emotional wellbeing was somewhere between
60,000 to 75,000 dollars, depending on where you lived. The
same study found life satisfaction plateaued at an average
income of 95,000 dollars around the world![14] This data was
based off of 1.7 million responses across 164 countries.

Of course, the incomes that brought the greatest wellbeing
and life satisfaction varied by country, depending on the cost
of living. For instance, life satisfaction plateaued at 105,000
dollars when only focusing on the USA.

The point of this study is not to focus on an exact income
threshold, but to appreciate that our obsession with constantly earning and acquiring *more* will not lead to the emotional wellbeing, happiness, and fulfillment we anticipate.

---

14   For those of you who like to know more about study design, the data was
     compiled from over 1.7 million individuals in 164 countries based on the
     Gallup World Poll. The salary figures were reported in US dollars on an
     individual basis, so income levels for families may differ. Additionally,
     purchasing power across countries were used to normalize results. Qual-
     itative questions related to wellbeing and life satisfaction were used to
     perform the regression analysis.

To further expand upon this notion of why *more* isn't always necessarily better, a 2005 article published by Drs. Lyubomirsky, Sheldon, and Schkade in *Review of General Psychology* explains that only 10 percent of our happiness is actually determined by our circumstances (job, car, house, salary, relationship, etc.). Yet, our circumstances are what we tend to focus our time, attention, and effort on when we don't feel happy.

Think about the last time you felt unhappy. What did you want to change in your life to make yourself feel better?

I know I'm often quick to blame my circumstances when things aren't going my way. I think, "If only I had a better job or more money, I wouldn't feel this way." But the science says that's not likely to bring us the happiness we're looking for.

So, if changing your circumstances won't bring about the happiness you want, what will?

The article goes on to say 40 percent of our happiness is actually determined by our mindset, everyday thoughts, and behaviors. Meanwhile, genetics account for a whopping 50 percent of our happiness![15] And while the exact percentage of happiness that is genetically determined varies depending

---

15   By digging deeper into the genetic component of happiness, a 1996 study by Drs. Lykken and Tellegen correlated happiness and genetics by assessing the wellbeing and reported happiness of approximately thirteen hundred sets of middle-aged twins using an assessment called the Multidimensional Personality Questionnaire. Both identical (monozygotic) and fraternal (dizygotic) twins were assessed for comparison. Astonishingly, in a smaller subset of the twin population, they were able to perform retests at 4.5- and 10-year intervals to assess stability and reproducibility of results over time.

on the research study you choose to cite, there is definite consensus genetics do play a factor.

HAPPINESS COMPONENTS

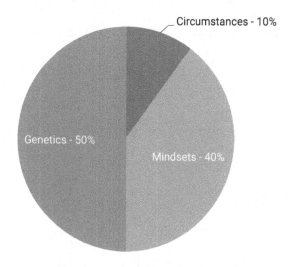

I had no idea happiness was a heritable trait!

So, does this mean we are doomed for unhappiness? I don't know about you, but I have some curmudgeons in my family tree. Lucky for us, the answer is a resounding *no.*

It turns out there are a lot of different things we can do mentally and behaviorally to feel happier over time. (Spoiler— that's what we'll dive into in Part Two of this book!) Ultimately, we can begin to reframe our thinking by seeing life as a journey, not a destination. Go ahead, groan at my use of the massively overused, cheesy expression, but the research and data prove it to be true.

With all of this in mind, it seems the unhappiness and negativity Terry was feeling after being offered the glamorous CMO role was perfectly explainable. The strange part of her story was just how quickly she came to realize this for herself. She didn't even accept her dream job for crying out loud!

Naturally, I had to learn about the valuable tools and tactics she had used to come to this realization so quickly. I wanted her cheat code for being able to reflect and reprioritize her goals.

So, Terry, do you have any tools or resources you can share with the readers?

"No. I'm extremely intuitive and…followed my gut."

Thanks, Terry. Very helpful.

In reality, this actually is a useful piece of advice because we all have an inner voice that speaks to us. However, some of us are better at listening to it than others. It just so happens Terry's intuition, her inner voice, is her superpower.

She attributes her uncanny ability to analyze, reflect, and adapt at lightning speed to her upbringing. By the time Terry was eleven years old, she had lived in forty different places! She literally attended a different school every year up until the fifth grade.

While others may have struggled with the constant change, Terry quickly learned how to assess each new environment to learn who the cool kids were, what to avoid in the cafeteria lunch line, and who to befriend to fend off bullies.

Okay, she didn't quite share that list with me, but it seems legitimate, doesn't it? But she did become very comfortable with change and extremely skilled at reading the room and assessing what unique dynamics were occurring at each school. This skillset has served her well as an adult when it comes to assessing career and personal opportunities.

After Terry turned down the CMO role, she eventually left her marketing job with the plan of taking some time off to rest, recharge, and reflect on how to proceed with her career, considering her North Star had now vanished. She asked herself two key questions: what am I good at and what do I like to do?

So, her career as an executive and career coach was born. She admitted it was not an easy transition given external societal pressures, but she noted, "It's hard, but it's authentic. People aren't necessarily going to look at me and be like, 'Hey, she's got her ticket punched...Look at her, she's the CMO.'" This concept of social comparisons and the pressures we feel is something we'll dive into in Part Two as well.

Every now and again, she needs to remind herself of the very principle she teaches her executive clients: "You don't have any business knowing what other people think of you." This sage advice is crucial in all of our own pursuits for success, as it is tempting to cave to what others expect or want from you. But in the end, by staying true to herself and listening to her gut, Terry has found a path that is providing her the freedom, impact, and happiness that allows her to consider herself successful.

Similarly, after some deep reflection following the financial crisis at AIG, Patrick realized, "I had made a lot of decisions without really calibrating them to what I was meant to be doing and what I wanted to be doing, mostly out of risk aversion. And in one fell swoop, because of external circumstances, they all crashed together. I needed to step back and deeply rethink what I was doing because it was stupid and I had the ability to change it."

He leveraged the money he had saved and took a sabbatical to focus on his wellbeing and figure out what was next for his professional career.

"I really didn't know what to do and I was very lost. I actually tried to go to job interviews for similar PE roles and every time I did, I left thinking, 'I can't do this again.' I hated all the jobs. I decided I was just going to be a freelancer and not commit to anything, and that led me to doing a bunch of freelancing projects or consulting projects. My decision was to not decide. My decision was to just not commit to anything and do a bunch of stuff because I was afraid of... getting back into private equity and being miserable. But I was also afraid of choosing the wrong thing and having it blow up in my face."

With all of this mixing and matching, he found his true calling: a diversified career portfolio that includes venture capital, advising start-ups, angel investing, philanthropy, serving on boards of directors, becoming an author, and taking on speaking engagements. He is a modern-day Renaissance man!

Funny enough, by not committing to any one career, Patrick was able to find the lifestyle that matched his own personal values and let him pursue a multitude of his passions.

That's not to say everything is always peachy, though. "I have to do shitty things sometimes, too, it's not like every day is sunshine and roses. But you know, I say to myself, 'This pays the bills so tomorrow I can spend the whole day working on my nonprofit work.'"

Like Terry, I asked Patrick for the strategies and tactics he used as he evaluated the opportunities he was presented with and the projects he decided to work on. And yet again, I got a similarly frustrating answer.

I questioned, "Is it a gut feeling?"

He replied, "Big time! I ask myself, 'Do I feel comfortable?' And a little discomfort is good because it means you're learning. But if I feel totally uncomfortable, I don't want to be there, which is why I'm not a good, 100-percent entrepreneur, because that's all about being uncomfortable all the time and I don't like discomfort."

Instead, he considers himself more of a 10-percent entrepreneur, which just so happens to be the title of his book.[16] With his diversified career portfolio, much like a diversified financial portfolio, his differentiated approach allows him to better weather any external circumstances or fluctuations in the market so he never has to relive his painful experience at AIG again.

---

16   I highly recommend reading *The 10% Entrepreneur: Live Your Startup Dream Without Quitting Your Day Job* for those of you who have found yourselves thinking about how to become a bit more entrepreneurial without necessarily diving into the deep end of entrepreneurship by quitting your day job to start your own business.

Patrick has found a plethora of opportunities that brings him freedom, fulfillment, and happiness. It's a true success story simply because those aspects align with his own personal priorities.

So much of Terry and Patrick's stories resonate with me due to my mentality and experiences in my twenties. If you recall from the Introduction, I once got four promotions in three years and still felt unhappy, underappreciated, and unfulfilled. Some of that was definitely due to hedonic adaptation, but a lot of it had to do with my frame of mind and misaligned lifestyle. I was almost entirely focused on my circumstances at that time of life, which meant I was neglecting 90 percent of the happiness equation!

I won't lie—despite having done all of this research and understanding more about what truly drives happiness, I still have to remind myself from time to time to appreciate the journey, not constantly want more, and avoid the curse of FOMO. Like I said, Redefining Success isn't easy and doesn't happen overnight, but learning from others and understanding the science sure does help!

KEY CHAPTER TAKEAWAYS

- Establishing goals and a vision for your own success is crucial, but your North Star can change over time as you continue to learn and evolve as a person.
- Reaching your North Star will not lead to happiness on its own. The science supports the cliché: it's about the journey, not the destination.

- Your circumstances (job, house, car, etc.) only account for 10 percent of the happiness equation. Meanwhile, your mindset accounts for 40 percent and is what you should truly focus on. (More on this in Part Two!)
- Trial and error is invaluable in your search for what you enjoy in life. Much in line with the growth mindset, you should be open to trying different jobs and activities until you find things you like.
- Focus on building a "career toolbox" with experiences and capabilities that translate to broader contexts. Once you understand your skills, you can then map them to what you like to do to identify future opportunities. If you identify a role or activity that requires different skillsets than what you currently have, you can focus your time and effort on acquiring those missing skills or experiences.
- Listen to your gut or inner voice! It's much more powerful than you give it credit for.
- You don't have any business knowing what other people think of you.

CHAPTER 4

From Climbing Ladders to Climbing Pyramids

Achieving Fulfillment Often Requires
Reaching Self-Actualization

"I had this ache, this feeling in my bones it wasn't right."

Meet Bill Novelli. At the time he felt this, he was quickly climbing the corporate ladder in the marketing world in what he likes to describe as the "*Mad Men*-era of marketing." That's right, think about Jon Hamm enjoying his three-martini lunch, a bottle of scotch in his desk, and an endless supply of power suits.[17] Note—I may have extrapolated a bit from Bill's description.

---

17 *Mad Men* is a television show that aired from 2007 to 2015. It was about "one of New York's most prestigious ad agencies at the beginning of the 1960s, focusing on one of the firm's most mysterious but extremely talented ad executives, Donald Draper." Donald Draper, played by Jon Hamm, epitomizes the cutthroat, elite ad agency life, but is perhaps better known for his constant smoking, drinking, and fooling around with his mistresses, even in the office (IMDb, 2021).

Yet, despite this enviable career position and trajectory, Bill was still uneased. This feeling despite having what society deems as "success" is something I personally can relate with all too well and is a common trend throughout our stories.

So, in hopes of finding his passion, Bill shifted roles to go work for an equally impressive ad agency. Yet, despite the change, the ache just kept growing until finally Bill got his wakeup call.

"I got back from a client meeting and I was working on two new products. One was a soft, moist, extruded dog food and the other one was a kid's cereal. And this young copywriter came into my office and he said, 'Hey, we're working on concept statements for the kid's cereal. Do you have any samples?' So, I reached into my briefcase and I took out a package of this soft, moist, extruded dog food and threw it across the room to him and I said, 'Yeah, here.' And he caught it and said, 'Yeah, we can sell this.' And it hit me. 'I've got to get out of this business.'"

Imagine that. You're working at a company, busting your butt trying to make creative ads for your clients. You are getting paid very well to help sell things like dog food and cereal. Yet, you are so apathetic about the work that the products are interchangeable. Perhaps even worse, your company is so good at what it does that your colleague has no issue with creating a kid's cereal advertisement using a sample of soft, moist, extruded dog food. Now, I've had some terrible cereal in my day, but even I couldn't stomach that!

This seems like the perfect time to introduce the notion of Maslow's hierarchy of needs because the bottom layer of the hierarchy has to do with our physiological needs, such as food (hopefully something tastier than dog food), water, clothing, etc.

Abraham Harold Maslow was a psychologist who pioneered self-actualization theory. In a nutshell, Maslow argued we all have a hierarchy of needs we want to satisfy. These needs range from the very basic necessities of life (i.e., physiological needs) to the highest order need of self-actualization (being the best we can be—sorry, US Army recruiting, Maslow had the idea first).[18] As we meet the needs of a particular level, our attention can then turn toward fulfilling the needs of the next step of the hierarchy (Maslow, 1943).

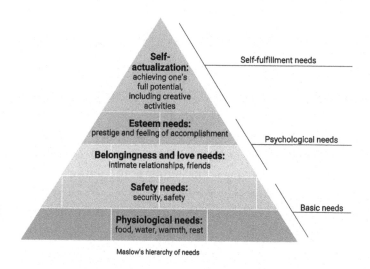

Maslow's hierarchy of needs

---

18 The US Army slogan, "Be all you can be," was first used during an advertisement during the 1981 New Year's college football games (Evans, 2021). I don't know about you, but I vividly remember seeing these commercials in the '90s. Who knew it was first aired in 1981?

For example, Maslow's hierarchy would stipulate that most of the time, if someone is starving or struggling to find food or shelter, that person would be concerned with basic survival and wouldn't have the capacity to worry about love or a sense of belonging. That's not to say the levels are always pursued in order, but individuals tend to gradually move from the bottom to the top.

Typically, individuals in the middle class or higher have the bottom two levels of the hierarchy under control and can focus on higher psychological needs such as building friendships, joining a community, building a network, finding a significant other, etc. Once those psychological needs are met, individuals then reach the self-actualization stage to live up to their own potential (Sullivan, 2019). I feel daunted just thinking about that!

Personally, I feel much of my twenties was spent waffling between the two psychological levels of belongingness and esteem. After graduating from Penn State with my undergraduate degree, I moved to Washington, DC for my new job and was establishing new friendships, dating my now wife, and attempting to build a professional network. Meanwhile, I was also doing everything in my power to become "accomplished" in my career and move up the metaphorical corporate ladder. I was putting an immense amount of pressure on myself to "live up to my potential" (whatever that means) and climb up the metaphorical rungs of society. I didn't know about Maslow's hierarchy at the time, but essentially, I was trying to reach that coveted self-actualization stage of life.

Let me tell you, reaching self-actualization is no easy feat. Frankly, it's something I continue to—and will always—struggle with. But I can tell you that through this book writing journey and by going through the exercises I outline in Part Two, my version of self-actualization has gotten much clearer in my mind.

Hopefully, this book will be helpful in your own quest to the top of Maslow's pyramid!

This progression I went through also fits Marissa Fernandez's story perfectly. Marissa is a wonderfully accomplished individual who I had the privilege of interviewing. It's amazing how many folks came out of the woodwork to share their stories with me for the creation of this book.

Similar to Bill's story, Marissa joined a Fortune 500 company early in her career as a marketer and started "climbing up the corporate ladder. I just sort of set the goal to become a chief marketing officer (CMO) because that's what I felt like I should do. Just like a first-grader goes to second grade and then third grade and eventually goes to high school, I just assumed ...I'm on this other ladder...I didn't even consider my path could be different. It just was like, 'Alright, chief marketing officer, here I come.'"

It almost sounds like there's a magical elevator that should take us all to these swanky job titles, except the elevator breaks down all the time and sometimes takes you to the wrong floor. I've certainly felt that way early in my career.

After years of marketing and a short stint in consulting to bolster her skillset, Marissa earned herself the role of vice president of marketing strategy and fan development for the National Football League (NFL). Being a big sports fan, that title sounds insanely cool to me! But it wasn't chief marketing officer, so Marissa kept hustling to make her CMO dream a reality.

One day, Marissa's dream finally came true: "I got a call from a recruiter about a chief marketing officer job here in New York at a golf and entertainment company. I was like, 'Oh my gosh! Sports and entertainment space—chief marketing officer. There's the title, great compensation—alright, this is it.' And I took the job and realized, 'Oh, I'm not immediately fulfilled.'"

Thud…another one bites the dust.

While Marissa kept working and hoping to gain an appreciation for her new role, the world was suddenly and drastically changed by COVID-19. In March 2020, like so many others throughout the globe, Marissa was laid off. This was an absolutely devastating event for Marissa, which just added to all of the stresses the pandemic brought. Yet, one of the main emotions Marissa felt was relief.

Relief? Is that a typo?

Nope, that's definitely not a typo. Marissa shared, "That was really the 'Oh Shit Moment' because I had never been unemployed. So much of my self-worth was tied up in being successful in my career, and to lose that felt like I didn't even have an identity anymore. I felt a range of emotions, but relief was one of them. That was an important emotion for me to feel because it was me starting to acknowledge my own desire, truth, and intuition. I realized in the majority of my career, I was thinking about this title as success and money as success. I realize now for myself, and with all of my clients, those things do not provide sustainable levels of fulfillment."

Marissa took the next year to really reflect and ponder what on earth she wanted for her life. Being a self-diagnosed "personal development junkie," Marissa read numerous self-help books, completed a plethora of associated workbook activities, began meditating, and joined support groups of like-minded, accomplished individuals who were undergoing a similar transition in life.

This was a personal struggle for her and took time! A key theme of this book is that truly reflecting on what you want and realigning your life accordingly is hard but incredibly rewarding.

Marissa explained, "For some people, a switch goes off and they're on a new path and that's amazing. But I think, for a lot of people, you're like, 'Am I on the ladder? Am I back off the ladder?' And being really forgiving, curious, and proud of yourself, even if it's messy, is important, and that's part of my story."

In the end, Marissa found her calling as a professional coach. She has found so much fulfillment in what she does that her North Star has now shifted. One day, she was contacted by a recruiter to become the chief operating officer for a major professional sports team. After nailing the first interview, she withdrew herself from candidacy because she realized it did not align with what she wanted anymore.

There's really only one word to describe that move: badass. It sounds like Marissa has climbed her way to the top of Maslow's hierarchy of needs pyramid if you ask me.

But what about our good friend, Bill Novelli? Did he ever find a way out from the dog food/kid's cereal advertising game?

Bill's calling finally came to him when he had the opportunity to attend a press conference being led by Joan Ganz Cooney in 1968. That happened to be the press conference in which the launch of *Sesame Street* was being announced.

That's right, the announcement of the TV show that revolutionized childhood learning. Again, just the fact Bill was in attendance for such a historic announcement goes to show how much Bill was crushing it at his job despite feeling so unsatisfied.

Because of Joan and *Sesame Street*, Bill came to realize, "You can use marketing to sell dog foods and cereal like I was, but you can also use it to sell issues, ideas, and causes like she was doing."

In reflection, it was clear Bill's career progression at that stage of his life was misaligned with his true priorities, leading to this feeling of unfulfillment and emptiness at work. The problem was not his career choice, because Bill loved marketing! Bill simply did not feel like he was using his marketing powers for good.

In my interview with Bill, he shared, "My epiphany was not to get work-life balance right; it was to get my career goal right. That made a big difference for me. My original goal as I was taking these Wharton marketing courses… was to get a job at a big company, climb the ladder, move into a corner office, make money, and retire. My new goal became to make significant contributions to solving major social problems."

Now, Bill didn't know this, but he was at the forefront of a global business movement. Today, companies with strong corporate social responsibility (CSR) initiatives surrounding making a positive difference in environmental, social, and corporate governance (ESG) are *thriving*.

Originally, companies focused on making a positive impact were thought to do so at the expense of profitability and long-term growth. However, Nielsen, a leader in market research and consumer insights, found 55 percent of global online consumers were willing to pay more for products or services from companies that were committed to positive and social-environmental impact (Nielsen, 2014). Additionally, these companies enjoy a stronger bond with their employees leading to better retention and employee satisfaction (Gross, 2021).

These efforts also apparently translate to long-term financial success for these companies. In a 2019 white paper, Morgan Stanley found investment funds that invested in companies with a strong focus on sustainability performed the same as, if not better than, traditional funds. Additionally, funds focused on sustainable companies provided lower downside risk than traditional funds regardless of the asset class.

At the time, though, Bill had no idea his new focus on making an impact and "doing well by doing good" would prove to be so personally rewarding and financially lucrative.

Armed with the realization that he wanted to use his marketing powers for good, Bill began his job search yet again and ended up taking a position with the Peace Corps as a director of advertising. It was a decision that entailed large sacrifices, including a sizeable pay decrease and the need to uproot his family from northern New Jersey to Washington, DC.[19]

Imagine your spouse comes home one day and says, "Hey, honey, I want to move us to Washington, DC for a new job. The kids will need to go to new schools. We need to sell our house and move away from our friends. Oh, by the way, I'm going to make less money too. Love you!" This is no small ask.

Bill admits, "It took a certain amount of courage, but I had a secret weapon, which was my wife. My wife is an adventurer. If I say to her, 'Let's go to the North Pole and study the ice core.' She'd say, 'Okay, let's do it.' I was lucky in that respect."

The power and impact of surrounding ourselves with the right people cannot be understated. Because with his wife onboard and his family on his side, this seemingly risky

---

19   It was at this point in our interview Bill shared a quote I absolutely loved. The quote is about the importance of seeking out growth opportunities and accepting change in life. "Consider the barnacle. The barnacle searches for a place to live and it then cements its head to a rock and it stays there for the rest of its life. We need to avoid the fate of the barnacle." —John Gardner

decision ended up leading to Bill's undeniably incredible career.

After moving to DC, Bill met his future business partner, Jack Porter, while working at the Peace Corps. Together, Bill and Jack cofounded Porter Novelli, a global PR agency dedicated to helping organizations find, live, and tell their purpose in order to thrive. They focused entirely on organizations that had ambitions to make a positive impact, motivate action, secure loyalty, and encourage advocacy to ultimately drive a healthier bottom line. Today, Porter Novelli has a worldwide presence with over seven hundred employees.

That new PR firm they created aligned perfectly with Bill's own priorities, leading to a sense of fulfillment. When the PR firm was eventually acquired and began to pivot away from the causes that mattered to Bill, he decided to depart in search of more impactful positions.

At that point, Bill went on to become CEO of the AARP (American Association for Retired Persons). Yes, that AARP—the organization that helps over forty million people over the age of fifty. He also founded the Campaign for Tobacco-Free Kids and Business for Impact at the Georgetown University McDonough School of Business.

Additionally, he served as the executive vice president of CARE, an international relief and development nonprofit, and currently works on the boards of directors for the American Cancer Society, the Coalition to Transform Advanced Care, Capital Caring Health, and Strategic Partnerships. The list of appointments and accolades seemingly goes on and on and on.

The man has found his calling—it is to leave a lasting legacy of positive impact on this world. Yet, none of this would have been possible without the tough decision to initially stop climbing the corporate ladder and take a pay cut in hopes of making a difference.

Because of his reflection, realization, and decision to pivot, Bill found more fulfillment, satisfaction, and happiness in his life—a true success story by any metric. Talk about self-actualization!

Throughout my interviews, I heard many amazing thoughts and quotes. One of my favorites came from my discussion with Marissa because she perfectly captured the essence of what it means to live in misalignment and the importance of Redefining Success for yourself.

"If you ask people, 'What are your values?' People are not going to say, 'My values are work, work, work, work, and work.' But if they're saying their values are their family and being in service to others, then you look at:

- *How do they spend their time?*
- *What keeps them up at night?*
- *How much energy are they giving to work?*
- *How much energy are they giving outside of work?*

If they're in a grind, chances are the answers to the questions don't reflect their internal metrics of success and they suggest they're focused very much, if not exclusively, on the external measures of success. It's ambitious, well-intentioned people who are set up to fail because they don't feel they have the capacity or permission to define success on their own terms."

—MARISSA FERNANDEZ

After Marissa said that so eloquently, I may or may not have suggested she write the rest of my book for me.

KEY CHAPTER TAKEAWAYS

- Keep your eyes and ears open for opportunities that will provide you with chances to grow personally and professionally. As you consider these opportunities for yourself, be sure to listen to your gut/inner voice.
- Do not underestimate the importance of trial and error. If you're not content with your current lifestyle, be open to trying new things that may better align with your priorities in life. While what you try may not be a perfect fit, it will at least inform your next decision.[20]
- Become a "personal development junkie" to learn about yourself and grow both personally and professionally.
- Meditation can be a helpful tool in the path to self-actualization. We'll explore the science of meditation as well as other useful tactics in Part Two of the book.

---

20 These first two takeaways sound awfully familiar, don't they? This author must be lazy! Well, maybe, but this was actually done on purpose. The importance of listening to and trusting your inner voice cannot be understated. All too often we hear that voice and elect not to do anything about it. Plus, they say on average, an adult needs to hear something seven times before it really sinks in! I won't repeat myself *that* much, but a little bit won't hurt.

- Joining communities of likeminded individuals can help to create a sense of belonging, understanding, and accountability as you think about your priorities and next steps in your life.

CHAPTER 5

Waiting Is Overrated

——

There's No Need to Wait, Redefine
Success Now to Reap the Rewards

Would I be happy doing what I'm doing ten years from now?
Go ahead, take a moment to answer the question for yourself.

I won't lie, I personally hate this type of question. It's the
classic interview question of "Where do you see yourself in
five to ten years?" Let's be honest, I don't even know what
I'm going to eat for lunch most days, let alone where I see
myself in five to ten years.

But in order to have a chance to take tangible steps toward
a future that excites you, you first need to define where you
want to go. Sounds a lot like the first step in Redefining Success for yourself, doesn't it?

Because of this book writing journey, I had the opportunity to interview Yanik Silver, one of the most profound and inspiring individuals I have ever had the pleasure of speaking with. Yanik is the author of *The Cosmic Journal*, a completely revolutionary publication that is 100 percent handwritten, with Yanik's own hand-drawn sketches included.[21]

The Cosmic Journal started as Yanik's own personal journal and morphed into a published book that is chockfull of sage advice, provocative writing prompts, inspirational exercises, and powerful messages about purpose. Here's an example of one page:

---

21 Personally, having gone through the book editing process, I can't imagine the time and energy it took to get his handwritten journal ready for publishing. Apparently, the editor would ask him to completely redraw certain images or handwrite certain words that were misspelled so they could be glued atop his previous work. Insane!

Following Your Heart is Frequently Scary... But Never Wrong

The Universe conspires with you to support you once you finally "jump." Only the times when you step to the edge and hesitate is there confusion. Your heart leads you to the path less taken. The path of trusting your inner guidance to nudge you to keep showing up in full service. For some reason, each time we follow heart, it seems scary until you realize you are fully supported every single time.

- ♡ -

I cannot recall one single time, with an elevated view, that I was ever upset I followed my heart. You cannot be mistaken in service of your built-in GPS. There is a certain strange PULL and allurement that simply will not quit. Your heart is that bridge between your cosmic blueprint and the perfect unfolding here. Now.

Q: What are you standing on the precipice of? Go ahead...

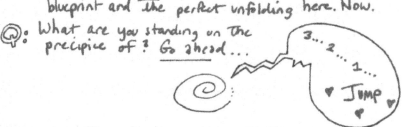

Like I said: my interview with Yanik was extremely profound and thought-provoking.

Yanik is the founder of Maverick1000, "an invitation only, global network of industry transforming entrepreneurs connecting in bold, new ways to challenge and collectively support each other's biggest business goals, engage in reinvigorating experiences, and co-create a worldwide multiplier impact (to date raising over three million dollars)."

But before Yanik became who he is today, his first claim to fame came from online marketing. The man had a gift! In a 2020 interview on Hal Elrod's *Achieve Your Goals* podcast, Yanik shared, "I had the Midas touch."[22]

He literally built seven seven-figure companies in his early career. He admits, "[I] really [didn't] know what the heck I was doing. No business planning, just following my instincts." If only we all had such lucrative "instincts."

---

22   If you're unfamiliar, the Midas touch comes from Greek mythology. King Midas was the "not-so-smart king of Phrygia." One day, King Midas showed compassion to Silenus, companion of the god of wine, Dionysus, who had drunkenly stumbled into King Midas' garden. As a reward, Dionysus granted King Midas one wish. Not being the brightest bulb, King Midas wished everything he touched would turn to gold. With his new wish granted, King Midas was ecstatic with his newfound endless wealth—hence the expression "the Midas touch."

Unfortunately, there is more to the story, which frankly makes the saying we use today a bit misleading. King Midas' demeanor quickly shifted when he became hungry and thirsty because any food or drink he touched would turn to gold in his mouth. He even accidentally killed his daughter by turning her to gold. Now seeing his newfound "gift" as a curse, King Midas ultimately begged Dionysus to have his wish reversed (The Editors of Encyclopaedia Britannica, 2021).

It turns out, like any story, there's more than meets the eye.

Yanik shared a bit about his childhood and early career in a 2013 episode of *Eventual Millionaire* with Jaime Tardy. His instincts actually began to develop at the ripe age of eleven, when he started helping out with his family's medical device repair business. Initially, Yanik helped with some odd jobs, but by the time he was fourteen, he was helping his father with telemarketing.

Can you imagine cold-calling doctors as a fourteen-year-old trying to convince them to use your medical device repair services? I know my prepubescent voice and speaking skills at that age would have instilled zero confidence for any doctor looking to have a medical device repaired. Let's be honest, the business likely would have gone bankrupt if it was in my hands! Yet, the business continued to grow thanks to Yanik's help.

At the age of sixteen, Yanik expanded his role and helped to transform the business into a national brand by teaching himself about advertising and direct response marketing. Additionally, he began implementing new marketing strategies for the company.

Yanik eventually leveraged all of these experiences into starting his own mailing and information publishing company. This was the first of many companies he founded, which led to his booming online marketing career and seven different seven-figure businesses. Could the Midas touch be an understatement?

Listening to Yanik's early career, what really stood out to me was he had a tremendous work ethic from a young age. In his interview with Jaime, he attributes some of this drive to the fact that he and his family immigrated to the United States when he was two years old. His family of four made the long journey to the USA with 256 dollars to their name.

My family also immigrated to the USA from very meager means, and I can tell you the American dream helps to cultivate a strong work ethic and appreciation for all you earn. In my case, it also meant interning at my dad's office as a teenager during my summers, helping with yardwork, and a heavy emphasis on education.

This kind of drive is something we can all aspire to better implement in our lives, no matter our nationality or origin story.

So, let's go back to our initial question: "Would I be happy doing what I'm doing ten years from now?" It just so happens this question radically changed Yanik Silver's life and helped him begin his transition to the impact maker he is today.

In our interview together, Yanik reflected, "That was sort of like a little cosmic alarm clock moment. The real answer was no. That sort of started me on this whole journey of exploring."

I really love Yanik's concept of the "cosmic alarm clock." As he describes it, "You get this little voice that's sort of whispering in your ear, especially for people who have been successful, in whatever way we define success, saying, 'Okay, what else?'"

I don't know about you, but this little voice has definitely popped up a few times in my life. Oftentimes, it would be during a long commute or after a particularly hard day at the office. But unfortunately, my younger self would typically hit the metaphorical snooze button on the cosmic alarm clock ringing in my head and simply tell myself tomorrow would be a better day.

But as Yanik said, every once in a while, "the universe will bonk you on the head. Whether it's health-wise, relationship-wise, financially—it's sending us a wakeup call. So, we can either wake up and lean into this cosmic alarm clock or hit snooze and ignore it, and then it feels like our soul is dying each day we're not doing what we're truly meant to be doing."

This is exactly what happened to me with my dad's passing!

This concept of being "bonked on the head" by the universe reminds me of another remarkable and inspiring individual I came across in my research: Arianna Huffington. Yes, the Arianna Huffington, the cofounder of *The Huffington Post* and now founder of Thrive Global. She also very well could be the poster child for the American dream. The woman has authored fifteen books for crying out loud; here I am struggling to finish one! The woman is an absolute icon.

Born in Greece, as the daughter of a newspaper owner, she went on to study at the University of Cambridge at the young age of sixteen. She later immigrated to the US in 1980 and began a series of political roles ranging from working on a senatorial campaign, covering the 1996 presidential election for Comedy Central, and even working for the likes of Bill Maher, host of the show *Politically Incorrect* (Albert, 2021).

This foundation of political knowledge led to her eventual gubernatorial campaign in the state of California. While she ultimately withdrew from the race, this just begins to paint the picture of the drive and ambition Arianna had early in her career.

When digging deeper into where this drive may have come from, it seems, like Yanik, it was baked into her DNA and further cultivated throughout her childhood. In a 2018 interview on Adam Grant's *WorkLife* podcast, Arianna shared, "My mother says for my fifth birthday party, I sent away all the children because they were interfering with my reading. I'm sure I was reading...coloring books, but whatever it was, I felt that was more important than socializing at that moment."

Think about it. Gifts, games, friends, attention, and cake! Would you be able to resist all of those temptations? I certainly could not. Which begs the question: what kind of five-year-old sends away friends from their own birthday party? The early makings of a truly great business leader with a love for learning and work.

Now, as you probably know by now, I am all about having your cake and eating it too. There is absolutely no part of me that would ever want to end a party early, especially not to go read. But what this is intended to show is that for some people, working provides a sense of joy. Arianna is one of those people.

In the interview with Adam Grant, Arianna openly admitted to being an "engaged workaholic." She shared, "I don't really have a distinction between my work and my life."

This prompted Adam Grant and his colleague, Nancy Rothbard (both University of Pennsylvania professors and researchers), to differentiate between unhappy workaholics and engaged workaholics. This distinction is quite important as "unhappy workaholics have higher risk for cardiovascular disease and diabetes," said Dr. Rothbard.

Additionally, unhappy workaholics tend to suffer from anxiety, stress, burnout, and mental illness. The toll of workplace stress is massive in the United States. Stanford researchers found workplace stress led to nearly 190 billion dollars of healthcare spending (8 percent of all US healthcare spending) and was attributed to nearly 120 thousand deaths each year (Moss, 2019). When expanded globally, the toll is even more drastic.

For those of you who are managers or aspire to be people leaders and need another financial reason to care, workplace stress costs the global workforce an estimated one trillion dollars in productivity each year. These are absolutely staggering numbers if you ask me!

But there is good news for you workaholics out there. It turns out there is a second classification of workaholic: the engaged workaholic. In her appearance on *WorkLife*, Dr. Rothbard elaborated, "People who do feel compulsion and some guilt when they're not working, but who also absolutely love their jobs, who are engaged in them, who are passionate about them, who find meaning in their jobs…for those folks who have both those kind of workaholic tendencies but also love their jobs, they're buffered from the negative [health] risk of workaholics."

So, in this case, the fact that work was very high on Arianna's priority list provided alignment with her workaholic lifestyle and meant she would be shielded from the physical, mental, and emotional toll that could come from workplace stress, anxiety, and burnout.

Or so she thought…

In 2007, shortly after being selected as one of *Time* magazine's top one hundred most influential people, Arianna woke up on the floor of her swanky New York City apartment in a pool of her own blood. Broken cheekbone, huge cut over her eye, and no memory of what happened—terrifying.

It turned out Arianna had literally almost worked herself to death.

In a 2016 interview at the Stanford Graduate School of Business, Arianna shared as she regained consciousness, "I literally thought to myself, 'Oh, so that's what success looks like.' Because it was such a juxtaposition of how I was doing in terms of the world's [perception] and how I was really doing."

What a powerful sentiment. There is so often a massive disconnect between the wellbeing of an individual due to perceived successes and the actual reality of his/her circumstances.

Arianna went on to share, "What led to my collapse in 2007 and my broken cheekbone…was I had completely bought into the collective delusion burnout was the way to achieve things. I had the delusion…nothing could be done except by me, and therefore, I had to be up all the time…[but ultimately] I feel very, very grateful… I honestly believe I would either be dead or have had a heart attack if I had continued that way."

As she said this last sentence during the interview, her demeanor shifted from one of grave seriousness to elation. It was clear to me she truly believed that moment was a massive turning point that saved her life.

Fortunately, following her fall, all of the diagnostic tests came back negative and indicated Arianna was perfectly healthy and simply overworked. Upon reflecting further, Arianna noted she had been working eighteen-hour days for quite some time and had neglected to consider the toll such a lifestyle could bring even to the "engaged workaholics" of the world.

So, in reflecting and prioritizing her wants and needs, Arianna admittedly did not want to change her work hours, workstyle, or priorities. However, she identified sleep as a powerful and necessary tool to enable her passion.

To go back to Arianna's quote about her work-life balance, her full thought was: "I don't really have a distinction between my work and my life, but I love it much more when I have taken time to recharge."

Arianna now makes it a point to get at least eight hours of sleep 95 percent of nights. Now, I know what you're thinking: "How the hell does Arianna Huffington get eight hours of sleep when I can barely fit in six?" Well, as is the case with anything, the key is prioritization and discipline. And let's be honest, if Arianna Huffington can do it, so can we if we really want to.

By understanding her needs and making crucial life changes, Arianna was able to continue to grow her *Huffington Post* empire to the crazy tune of a 315-million-dollar acquisition by AOL in 2011. From there, she went on to launch her new passion project: Thrive Global.[23]

It took a scary, blood-soaked moment for Arianna to realize the importance of looking at her life holistically and identify the right tools and tactics to allow her to live the lifestyle she wanted and enjoyed. In the end, her work

---

23 Thrive Global is dedicated to "ending the epidemic of stress and burnout." As you can see, Arianna took her experience with a serious health event, her own "Oh Shit Moment," and created a company to prevent the same from happening to others. How great is that? As you can tell, I really like this new company of hers—so much so that I am a contributing author to the site. How about that for shameless self-promotion?

continued to be one of the aspects that brought her the most joy. So, while a major pivot was not needed, a rebalancing of her life was necessary to enable her to continue her self-described "engaged workaholic" ways in a healthy and sustainable way.

Despite the positive outcome, even Arianna Huffington was not immune to the effects of living in misalignment. It's an unfortunate reminder that it usually takes something drastic to make us listen to our cosmic alarm clock ringing and reassess our life choices. Hopefully, this book convinces you to listen to that little voice and not hit that snooze button when you hear the cosmic alarm ringing in your own life!

Fortunately for us, there is another way.

Yanik Silver (remember him?) happens to have written about the concept of duality in his *Cosmic Journal*. Duality is the idea that oftentimes there are polarizing or even opposite sides to a given topic. Good vs. evil, heads vs. tails, yin vs. yang, Philadelphia Flyers vs. Pittsburgh Penguins. Alright, that last one may not quite fit the mold, but I had to give myself a way to say, "Go Flyers!"

TWO

This world is seemingly designed on the concept of polarity and duality. To experience cold you need warmth. For hunger there is fullness. To be in a relationship shows us the contrast and reflection. Our light side also has a shadow side. These two aspects are interwined in harmony, back and forth. The perfect paradox.

Male and female represent different aspects of our essence. Not just gender but energy. Push. Pull. Active. Receptive. The dance of universal forces. Finding that beautiful balance between the two sides.

Creating the balance of opposing forces in cooperation.

- Effortless Effort -

The narrative too many of us have been told is one side is right. One view is correct. One way to get where you want to. One side wants to blame the other in politics, in relationships, in agreements. Peace comes from bridging the polarity and seemingly opposite views + ideas.

Two asks us to look in the mirror and see the "other" in ourselves. What attracts us and what repels us? What do we appreciate about the "other" and ourselves?

Everything is in CONNECTION — ONE to the OTHER.

Left ⟷ Right
Modern ⟷ Ancient
Heart ⟷ Head
Commerce ⟷ Impact
Logic ⟷ Intuition
Spirit ⟷ Science
Receive ⟷ Give
Male ⟷ Female
Attraction ⟷ Repulsion
Light ⟷ Shadow

I would add to this list: those who wait for an "Oh Shit Moment" to reassess their lives and Redefine Success while they attempt to pick up the pieces of whatever chaos life threw their way vs. those who proactively Redefine Success for themselves on a consistent basis by listening to the cosmic alarm clock when it rings.

I'm not suggesting we can avoid "Oh Shit Moments" altogether (more on this in Chapter Seven). However, I am saying we should continuously be evaluating what matters to us and ensuring our choices and lifestyles are in alignment with those priorities to maximize our happiness, fulfillment, and ability to bounce back during tough times.

We should do our best to follow Yanik's example, as he was perceptive enough to listen to his cosmic alarm clock ringing before any major "bonking" took place. By being perceptive, Yanik was better positioned to deal with whatever "bonks" the world would send his way later in life.

Despite all of his financial and career accomplishments in digital marketing, in an interview with Garrett Gunderson in 2015, Yanik recalled thinking, "I had a great reputation, I was making a lot of money, and I had a great family. I probably should've been happy, but there was this nagging feeling I think a lot of entrepreneurs experience—this feeling or nudge you're being called to something greater. And the less we heed it, the louder it usually becomes."

This feeling is not limited to the entrepreneurial community. From my research, interviews, conversations with peers, and own personal experience, I can tell you this nagging feeling

Yanik explains is commonly experienced by doctors, teachers, lawyers, students, engineers, scientists, professors, sales people, data analysts, etc., etc., etc.

Let's be honest, you have probably felt this way at some point in your life as well. The question is, did you do anything to address that feeling?

For Yanik, doing something greater meant building an adventure travel company for likeminded entrepreneurs. Or so he thought...

In our interview together, he explained, "We ended up losing about forty thousand dollars. I was like, 'Ah, you know, it's an investment.' Then after about four hundred thousand dollars, my wife was like, 'What the hell are you doing?' That was one of these 'Oh Shit Moments' you're talking about. A lot of people think once you're successful, it should be so much easier, but really, then you get wrapped up in your self-worth being tied to your net worth. You get wrapped up in this identity of being a successful entrepreneur.

"And sometimes it's easier to do things when you're kind of an unknown or when you don't have as much reputation at stake. I could have easily gone back into my other world and continued to do digital marketing stuff, but that's really when I felt like my soul would be dying each day. So, my 'why' had to get bigger. My 'why' wasn't building [an] adventure travel company; it was to change the way businesses played."

So, armed with his new "why" and realization his net worth and self-worth were not connected, Yanik ended up selling his Aston Martin (I'm not kidding, in his early career he literally might as well have been King Midas) to make his new dream a reality.

He aspired to create an entrepreneurial network that would encourage entrepreneurs to "connect your head, your heart, [and] your higher purpose." So Maverick1000 was born. The man's ultimate goal is "to light one thousand suns who each have the potential to light another one thousand suns."

That's one million individuals he wants to impact with his life!

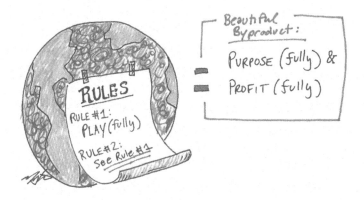

Don't get me wrong, despite losing the Aston Martin, Yanik still has some serious connections from his past life. One of his close friends is Richard Branson for crying out loud! And yes, being the adventure junkie he is, Yanik already has his ticket to go into space via Virgin Galactic.

As priorities and interests can change, Yanik remains a huge proponent of journaling, meditating, and experimenting with new habits to really understand his feelings, thoughts, and priorities in life—many of which I've personally used and will highlight in Part Two as we work to Redefine Success for ourselves!

When in doubt, Yanik likes to ask himself a simple question to identify if he is headed in the right direction: "What would my 111-year-old self tell me?"

KEY CHAPTER TAKEAWAYS

- Oftentimes, our gut or inner voice provides an early indication something is wrong and we may be heading down the wrong path in life. Listen to this voice and take time to reflect on what is causing this "cosmic alarm clock" to sound—don't hit snooze and wait for an "Oh Shit Moment!"
- Redefining Success requires reflection of what truly matters to us. Once we have those aspects identified, the key is to have discipline and prioritize those important aspects for ourselves.
- It's vital to view success with a holistic lens. Our efforts to reach top-of-the-pyramid self-actualization should not come at the expense of bottom-of-the-pyramid self-care (hey there, Maslow). Think about Arianna with her sleep! With this more comprehensive view, we can rebalance our lives to enable a healthy and sustainable route toward greater happiness and fulfillment.
- Understand your own "why." What are you motivated by? Why do you want the things you want?
- Answering seemingly simple questions can have a profound impact on your life by forcing yourself to really reflect. Examples include:
  - Would I be happy doing what I'm doing ten years from now?
  - What would my 111-year-old self tell me?

CHAPTER 6

The Never-Ending Job

Our Definition for Success Evolves over
Time, and So Our Job Is Never Done

Imagine the pristine Rocky Mountains. Beautiful snow covers every inch of the craggy peaks. Deafening quietness comes from being immersed by snow. It truly feels like unspoiled earth. The air even smells fresher and feels crisper as it fills your lungs.

Thinking about being in the beautiful Rocky Mountains during winter just makes me want to sit next to a toasty fire in a wooden lodge and enjoy good food, a nice, warm drink, and good company. Now, you may be thinking, "I don't have to travel all the way to the Rockies to partake in something like that—wooden lodges are ubiquitous across the northern US." That's fair, so let's up the ante a bit.

Along the western edge of the Rockies lies the Wasatch Range, home of stunning Park City, Utah. Even if you have never been there, you probably have heard of Park City due to its immaculate ski slopes. Just south of Utah Olympic Park, home of the 2002 Winter Olympics, Park City is a tranquil town of eight thousand residents and home to some of the best skiing in the United States. Every year, this tiny town welcomes six hundred thousand tourists as they flock to this impeccable skiing destination (Meet in Park City, 2017).

Of course, I've saved the best for last. What if I told you that tucked away at the bottom of the ski slopes in Park City is the only ski-in gastro-distillery serving some of the best rye whiskey you will ever taste: High West Distillery.

I personally first tried High West Whiskey back in 2016 when I was given a bottle of their flagship product, Rendezvous Rye, as a gift by my mentor and good friend, Chris. It instantly became a favorite of mine and a staple in my liquor cabinet.

Even my wife, who is the furthest thing from a whiskey person, took a sip and only slightly puckered her lips while saying, "I can see why someone would like it." That's huge praise from a non-whiskey person! So naturally, when I had the opportunity to reach out to David Perkins, the founder of High West Distillery, through a shared connection, I jumped at the chance.

In hindsight, you could say David was destined to open a distillery one day. David was a biochemist by training and always knew he wanted to start his own company someday. He also happened to enjoy whiskey quite a bit and married Jane, whose family was in the whiskey making business for three generations from the 1840s to 1915 until the pesky Prohibition shut down the family business.

Despite all of these now seemingly obvious signs, I still find myself fascinated by David's story due to what he gave up to make High West Distillery a reality. More impressively, it was how he was constantly reflecting and realigning his lifestyle to ensure he was living true to his values and priorities along the way.

You see, after David graduated with his degree in biochemistry from the University of Virginia, he worked in a laboratory for some years before eventually pursuing his MBA from Dartmouth. Quite the college pedigree, if I may say so myself.

Now armed with business prowess to go along with his technical background, he was recruited to the lucrative biopharmaceutical industry. David spent eight years at Amgen in various marketing functions followed by six years of commercial operations work at Genentech. Both of these companies were thriving at the time David was there. And like any good company, they were desperate to retain talent.

So, we introduce one of the hurdles in David's fabled tale: the golden handcuffs.

For those who may be unfamiliar, the golden handcuffs are "a collection of financial incentives that are intended to encourage employees to remain with a company for a stipulated period of time. Golden handcuffs are offered by employers to existing key employees as a means of holding onto them as well as to increase employee retention rates" (Kenton, 2021).

These incentives can be in the form of large, long-term performance bonuses, stock options, or other lavish perks.

Essentially, a company gives a whole lot of reasons as to why an individual should not leave the company. Because if the individual chooses to leave, they will be giving up a boatload of money.

Obviously, this is a fantastic problem for an individual to have. But paradoxically, most people view the golden hand-cuffs as a curse, as they often lead to a feeling of being trapped. If only we could all be so fortunate!

What is fascinating to me about David's story is his mindset from the start was drastically different and refreshingly positive when it came to the golden handcuffs. In our interview together, he shared, "I was fortunate I could forego salary. I left as much money on the table as I left with."

In other words, despite losing about 50 percent of his potential compensation (due to non-vested stock options, long-term bonuses that hadn't kicked in, etc.) with his decision to leave the company, the compensation he left with afforded him the opportunity to follow his passion. This is drastically opposed to the view that his lost compensation was a reason not to jump ship and follow his dreams. Seems like the classic glass is half full vs. glass is half empty mindset.

This highlights the power of understanding your priorities and why you earn money to begin with!

When diving deeper into his rationale, David reflected, "Passion is something that makes you jump out of bed in the morning. It's something you really enjoy. I like jumping out of bed in the morning. We all have hard days at work, and toward the end of my time in biopharma, I found myself jumping out of bed four or five days a week. So, I thought if I started my own thing, I could change that to be seven days a week. And it happened; I found my passion."

To recap, David saw the money he earned as a means to pursue his passion and increase the number of days he was excited to get out of bed. Now *that* sounds like a great use of money if you ask me.

This takes us to his inspiration story for founding High West Distillery. Like any good American whiskey story, this one takes place on the infamous Kentucky Bourbon Trail.[24]

David was in Louisville, Kentucky, for a wedding and decided to take a tour of the Maker's Mark Distillery. If you've never been, I highly recommend the trip, as the distillery grounds feel like a very old-timey town.

A light bulb went off instantly in David's head! Distilling bourbon is effectively biochemistry with a tasty end product. David realized he could combine all of his favorite aspects from his work experiences (biochemistry, marketing, and running an enterprise) into one singular business.

---

24 The Kentucky Bourbon trail consists of eighteen different distilleries which produce 95 percent of the world's bourbon. For all you non-whiskey fans, bourbon is a classification of whiskey. Therefore, all bourbons are whiskeys, but not all whiskeys are bourbons. For a whiskey to be considered a bourbon, it must "be made with a minimum of 51 percent corn, aged in new, charred oak containers, stored at no more than 125 proof, and bottled at no less than 80 proof" (Kentucky Bourbon Trail, 2021).

"For me, I had a lot of passion in my first job, a bench job in College Park, Maryland, with a diagnostics company doing DNA isolations. I really liked that stuff. To be able to do that same kind of stuff and make whiskey, it kind of was always there in a way." With a few short conversations with his wife and now business partner, David and Jane uprooted the family from San Francisco to Park City to start this new adventure of theirs in 2004.

Now I don't know about you, but as I was hearing David's story, I was thinking to myself, "Who on earth would be crazy enough to set up a distillery in Utah?"

In case you don't know, Utah is home to over two million Mormons (about 62 percent of the state's population in 2021) and this population typically does not consume *any* alcohol (World Population Review, 2021). And David's idea was to make and sell whiskey there? I thought this guy went to a fancy business school?

Well, clearly, David was onto something.

Very much in line with his personality and value-based decision-making process, David and his wife created a mission statement that was short and to the point. "To make delicious whiskey, to share our love of whiskey with our customers, and to celebrate our home, the West."

David went on to explain, "Sometimes we summarized this into 'Because Whiskey Matters.'" Beautiful, elegant, and simple.

It was with this mission statement that High West cultivated a strong culture and companywide passion that turned out to be pretty damn important in the end. David recalled, "Passion was the currency for us when the bank account was low." And while David admits it was a ton of work, ultimately, he ended up selling High West Distillery to the tune of a cool 160 million dollars in 2016. Anyone else's jaw on the floor by this point?

But even the way David decided to sell the company was aligned with his values! When asked if the acquirer would change operations or affect the end product in any way, David replied, "We wouldn't have been interested in talking to [Constellation Brands] if that was the case."

Is there anything this guy does without ensuring it is aligned with his own priorities? Well, the answer is clearly an emphatic "no."

I would argue that is the precise reason why David is so accomplished, down to earth, and happy as he tells his story. As he told me about the highs and lows of his journey, David emphasized his family was with him every step of the way.

Throughout his decision-making process, David kept his family at the forefront of each decision because he clearly knew his family was his top priority. David said, "My family grounds me and reminds me of what is important to me."

No matter how busy he got at any of his jobs or in launching the distillery, he always prioritized family time. Early on, David took the time to identify his own personal priorities and made each decision along the way with these priorities in mind.

As someone whose family is at the top of my own priority list, I found it refreshing and admirable to hear David emphasize the importance of his family all along his journey. Juggling family and career ambition is insanely difficult. It's so easy to simply focus on our career growth and tell ourselves it's all for our family. Our focus is well-intentioned but can ultimately lead us astray. While we all sometimes have to make sacrifices to fulfill our responsibilities and pay the bills, I feel it is imperative to continuously reflect and remind ourselves why we do the things we do to ensure we remain well-balanced and headed in the right direction. Hence, the point of this book!

To add to David's continued legacy, he now advises a rum company in Hawaii and has a bona fide business excuse to visit Hawaii regularly. How ridiculously awesome is that?

David used his love of biochemistry and business prowess to build a whiskey empire in a very thoughtful and inspiring way that ensured his decision-making process prioritized his family and his passions every step of the way. This consistency in aligning his life with his priorities is what led to him eagerly jumping out of bed seven days a week. Now that's success if you ask me, something I think we should all strive for.

Time for a little quiz. For each round, answer the following question:

WHO IS MORE SUCCESSFUL?

Question 1:
- Investment banker
- Artist
- Engineer
- T-shirt maker
- Doctor
- Teacher

Question 2:
- Someone making 100,000 dollars a year working eighty hours per week with average benefits
- Someone making 40,000 dollars a year working forty hours per week with fantastic benefits
- Someone making 200,000 dollars a year working one hundred hours per week with mediocre benefits
- Someone making 75,000 dollars a year working fifty hours per week with bad benefits
- Someone making 90,000 dollars a year working forty-five hours per week with good benefits

Question 3:
- Someone who is married with kids, owns a house, and is not very involved in the community
- Someone who is single, rents an apartment, and is heavily involved in the community

- Someone who has a significant other, lives with three roommates in an apartment, and has no hobbies or other community involvement
- Someone who is recently divorced, rents a house, and partakes in a number of hobbies with friends
- Someone who is in a polyamorous relationship, lives with their parents, and participates in a few leagues and community events

Question 4:
- Someone who is generally miserable
- Someone who is generally happy

Answers: No matter what you answered, I can tell you there are no right or wrong answers for Questions 1–3. Of course, Question 4 was meant to be an easy one. Didn't you just love these types of easy questions on tests in school? Hopefully, you would agree being happy is better than being miserable!

Due to societal norms and pressures, many of us are raised to believe that a more prestigious, stable job with higher pay is better and that we all should aspire to be married with kids in a house that we own. But that certainly is not what everyone wants.

Whether we do it consciously or subconsciously, societal norms and our upbringing are likely to have more people respond that an investment banker, engineer, or doctor is more successful than a teacher, artist, or T-shirt maker. Similarly, the person making 200,000 a year is more successful than the one making 40,000 a year.

Most of us are guilty of it, but in order to Redefine Success, we must break free from simply thinking more is better. More power, more fame, more money—that sounds a lot like my teenage definition of success from the Introduction!

It's time we evolve and Redefine Success because, in reality, life is complicated. Every decision we make has tradeoffs. Every job provides many different forms of "currencies" that are nearly impossible to weigh on an absolute basis, as the weight of each component is highly reliant on each individual's preferences—things like hours worked, salary, insurance coverage, impact, vacation, opportunities for growth, flexibility, stability, autonomy, remote work capability, childcare options, tuition reimbursement, legacy, parental leave, etc.

Sure, you want all of these aspects to be fantastic and top-notch. But the unfortunate truth is that everything in life comes with pros and cons.

Similar lists of "currencies" and associated tradeoffs could be listed for relationship status, community involvement, owning vs. renting vs. living with parents, number of hobbies, etc. The answer to the question "what is the right combination" is highly reliant on you.

As such, the right answers for the first three questions of the quiz would be entirely dependent on someone's personal preferences and whether that person was happy with what they were doing, felt fulfilled, and was living life aligned with their priorities.

For some people, the realization of tradeoffs comes seemingly naturally. Jonny Weitz, commercial banker turned T-shirt design mogul, just so happens to be one of the people who understood the notion of prioritization and tradeoffs early in life.

Despite only being in his twenties, Jonny seems to have hacked into this game we call life to clearly see through the systems and pressures society has thrown his way.

Initially, like me during my high school and early college years, Jonny wanted to become a doctor and practice medicine.[25] But in reflecting during our interview together, he realized his reasons for doing so were not so great. "Those people make a lot of money. The decision wasn't about the passion for science...but ultimately, I didn't find it interesting and it's a ton of work." Goodbye, medical school.

He then did what many kids do—he looked up to his older sibling for inspiration. Jonny's older brother was studying at the Ivey Business School, so off Jonny went to study business. "Having a business background opens up a lot of opportunities. You can take the business aspects and then apply it to literally anything."

Speaking from personal experience, while business school certainly does open a ton of doors, in reality, these programs are

---

25 Embarrassingly enough, the reason I decided not to pursue medicine is I fainted not once, but twice while observing medical procedures! After the second instance of waking up cold and clammy on a hospital floor and inadvertently becoming a patient, I decided it was time to hang up my metaphorical, nonexistent stethoscope to help improve patient outcomes through the development of innovative products and medicines.

incentivized to push students toward high-earning professions like investment banking and consulting to help boost the program's earnings statistics and allow the program to rise up the MBA rankings. But despite this pressure, Jonny again reflected and realized these professions were not exactly for him.

"The concept of investment banking still doesn't make sense to me. I went into commercial banking because there was o percent chance I was going to...work until three o'clock at night."[26] Jonny has mastered the art of understanding societal pressures and finding ways to appease them while still focusing on his priorities.

In this case, Jonny realized, "Society in school is telling me to do banking, so maybe I'll just take the commercial banking route. It's a bit of a mix without the grind. This is still what society's telling me to do—I'm still able to make money, get out, and have a bit of a balance with a social life."

But despite the pay and stability, commercial banking wasn't fulfilling for him. He continued to work at the bank for two

---

26 If you're an investment banker, then the crazy hours are no shock to you. But in case you're unaware of how rigorous investment banking can be, there was a scandal that surfaced in March 2021 in which a report was leaked indicating junior staff at Goldman Sachs were complaining about their deteriorating mental and physical health due to having to work one-hundred-hour work weeks! Employees were quoted saying, "The sleep deprivation, the treatment by senior bankers, the mental and physical stress...I've been through foster care and this is arguably worse."
   "Being unemployed is less frightening to me than what my body might succumb to if I keep up this lifestyle."
   "What is not okay to me is 110 to 120 hours over the course of a week! The math is simple; that leaves four hours a day for eating, sleeping, showering, bathroom, and general transition time. This is beyond the level of 'hardworking'; this is inhumane/abuse" (Williams-Grut, 2021). Ouch!

years, and despite not hating the work, found himself constantly asking, "What's next?"

As he pondered next steps, he began to build a side hustle around printing T-shirts. Initially, he was printing his shirts on a friend's garment printing machine to learn the ropes. But after some time improving his abilities and researching the available business opportunities, he decided to buy his own machine and set up a workshop in his parents' garage.

By starting his passion project on the side, Jonny was able to de-risk his next step while still taking tangible steps toward the lifestyle and career pivot he wanted.

During the height of the COVID-19 pandemic, Jonny decided to quit his job at the bank. "If I need to live in my parents' house for another year, I'll do it. That will be a tradeoff for me to become happier. Do I want to be twenty-six or twenty-seven years old living at home and single? No. But in life, you can't have a win at all times. So maybe at this point in my life, I'll take the career improvement as a win."

So, despite being colorblind, Jonny made the fulltime jump to designing and printing T-shirts for a living. Armed only with Photoshop skills he learned in high school, a business degree, and a self-proclaimed eye for stylish things, Jonny created his company—Grace Court. Now I'm no expert, but this endeavor doesn't sound like something I would be overly eager to invest in. But boy, would I have been wrong.

Jonny's designs have taken off! NBA players like Caris LeVert, Tyrese Maxey, Hamidou Diallo, Bruce Brown Jr., and Terance

Mann have all worn and promoted Jonny's vintage T-shirts. Jonny's products have done so well he was featured in *GQ* magazine![27]

Ultimately, Jonny's decisions were all about understanding his priorities in life and weighing the associated tradeoffs with pursuing a given path. All too often, we feel trapped in a given role because of time we've already invested. However, this is a sunk cost fallacy because the past cannot be changed.

In case you're unfamiliar, the sunk cost fallacy is when someone has the "tendency to continue an endeavor once an investment in money, effort, or time has been made" (Arkes, 1985). This is regardless of whether you've had positive or negative results to date.

As an example, let's say you decide to pay extra to get the supersized combo meal at a given restaurant. Halfway through eating this meal, you realize you are disgustingly full and are no longer enjoying the meal. Do you stop eating?

For those of you who thought, "Yes," congrats! You've extracted all of the value of the money you spent.

---

27 Straight from the *GQ* article that featured Jonny in 2021, Calum Marsh writes, "Loaded with bright, garish colors and intentionally gaudy type-faces, they're [T-shirts] meant to look like they came from the back of a rack in a market in Chinatown circa 1998. It's vintage bootleg kitsch—the flashier and more lurid, the better...Weitz's extremely (and charmingly) amateur designs, which he creates himself at home on his computer, look like a combination of homemade trading cards and high school graduation photos circa 1993—a whole lot of dorky, out-of-context pics layered on top of one another haphazardly." Say what you want, but that's seriously cool!

For those of you who thought, "No way, I need to keep eating because I spent money on this meal," this is the sunk cost fallacy in action.

The money you spent to supersize the meal is already spent, but you want to get your money's worth and keep eating despite not enjoying your meal anymore and potentially making yourself sick.

The same could be said about a specific job or career choice. If your job no longer brings you happiness and fulfillment, it may be time to reconsider your choice, no matter how much time you've "invested" in getting to your current role. In the end, it's all about understanding the tradeoffs.

In our interview together, Jonny really boiled down the issue back to our definition for success as teenagers: "People are focused on, 'How can I make the most amount of money?' 'How can I have a job title that sounds great so I can tell my friends…and so my parents can tell their friends?' A lot of it comes back to when you're fifteen. Middle school to high school to university, those are the steps that lead to your career path, right? You basically have to decide what you want to do as a fifteen-year-old. At that stage of life, you're not a conscious individual who's really thinking down the line."

While only one facet of life, the reality is that our choice of job affects nearly every aspect of our life. But as we've already learned, it's not realistic to think our priorities or definition for success will remain unchanged throughout our lives.

For David Perkins, this meant keeping his family at the forefront of every career decision he made by transitioning from public sector bench biochemist to MBA-trained biotech marketing guru, to a stint in commercial operations, to start-up whiskey distiller, to rum making advisor.

For Jonny, this meant eschewing medicine for business, undertaking a commercial banking role, starting a T-shirt printing side hustle, and ultimately becoming a fashion icon.

But that doesn't mean David and Jonny are done, that they no longer need to reflect because they've found their calling. Because in the end, we all continuously grow, adapt, and evolve throughout our lives. As such, our priorities in life also change over time.

It's because of this that our job is never done. We should regularly reflect on what matters to us, what brings us happiness, and what brings us fulfillment. We should be consistently Redefining Success for ourselves!

The good news is that gone are the days of having to spend your forty-year career at the same company. Sure, that's still possible if you want it, but according to the Bureau of Labor Statistics in 2020, the median employee now only spends 4.1 years at a given company.

If you find yourself in a job that isn't bringing you happiness and fulfillment anymore, we are fortunate to now live in the era of job hopping, redefining ourselves, and having endless networking and learning opportunities at our fingertips thanks to technology. While my examples in this chapter focus heavily on career, the same reprioritization can take place across all facets of life as you meet new individuals, are exposed to new experiences, find passions or hobbies, and continue along your own personal development journey.

KEY CHAPTER TAKEAWAYS

- Build a "career toolbox" that enables you to leverage skills in a variety of roles. A "career toolbox" is a set of skillsets and competencies you learn and understand. By investing time, energy, and resources in your own personal and professional development, you not only grow as an individual, but also make yourself more marketable and likely to prosper when you find the right opportunities for yourself.
    - Example: Despite having an entrepreneurial itch from an early age, David focused on learning, building skills, and creating some financial security to enable a future opportunity down the line. Without his time learning and creating a "career toolbox" as a bench scientist and subsequent biopharma marketer, High West Distillery would not have been possible.
- It is crucial to understand your values and priorities in life in order to make decisions that align with what matters to you. Otherwise, no matter how much you accomplish, you are likely to feel unhappy and unfulfilled.
- Every decision in life comes with tradeoffs. Only by understanding our priorities and the associated pros and cons of our decisions can we make the decisions that are most aligned with our priorities to maximize our happiness and fulfillment.

- One way to de-risk our actions is to take gradual steps toward a desired change. Instead of jumping head first into a new endeavor and quitting your day job, you can take small steps on the side to allow yourself time to learn and grow.
  - Example: Despite knowing he was unhappy with banking, Jonny began his career transition by starting a side hustle to learn more about the industry and craft.
- The sunk cost fallacy can cause us to continue to invest our resources (time, money, and effort) in things that no longer provide value to us. In the end, any resources spent in the past will not be recovered and our decisions should focus on the future.

CHAPTER 7

Life Pivots: The New Normal

Life Pivots Are a Central Part of Life Everyone
Will Need to Master Eventually

"The idea we'll have one job, one relationship, one source of happiness is hopelessly outdated. We all feel unnerved by this upheaval. We're concerned our lives are not what we expected, that we've veered off course, living life out of order. But we're not alone."

—BRUCE FEILER

A major theme in Part One of this book has been that all of the impressive individuals I've featured have made a major pivot in their lives in the pursuit of greater alignment with their own personal priorities.

Arianna Huffington experienced an involuntary pivot caused by a medical issue. Waking up in a pool of your own blood would rattle any of us, make us rethink our current lifestyle, and seek better balance!

Marissa Fernandez faced the unpleasant reality of being involuntarily laid off due to a pandemic ravishing the world. She was left asking herself, "What's next?" And she ultimately found a new North Star in coaching.

However, for many in this book, the pivot was voluntary. For Matthew Berry and Mike O'Donnell, this meant leaving the security of a steady paycheck to chase happiness through new pursuits in the fantasy football and barbeque industries, respectively. For Bill Novelli and Yanik Silver, a pivot was used to seek greater impact and legacy. Bill transitioned from *Mad Men*-era marketing to social impact while Yanik looked to inspire one million individuals through his work.

But maybe you're thinking to yourself, "Okay, good for those folks. But why do I need better alignment? I certainly don't need to pivot—my life is perfect!"

If you feel that way, then I applaud you and ask that you reach out to me to share your secret sauce to life. But the unfortunate reality is that pivots have become the new normal in life, voluntary or not.

To dive a bit deeper into the matter, I would like to introduce you to Bruce Feiler, author of seven *New York Times* bestselling books. Bruce's own story is fascinating! Like many of us in our twenties, Bruce felt like he had figured out this game we call life.

That is, of course, until life presented him with a rude awakening—his own "Oh Shit Moment."

In a 2020 interview on NPR, Bruce shared, "I discovered what I wanted to do early in my life. I had some success, I got married, I had children. And then I just got walloped by life. I got cancer, I almost went bankrupt, and my dad, who has Parkinson's, tried to take his own life multiple times."

But Bruce leveraged his difficult experience into his next passion project, his book *Life Is in the Transition: Mastering Change at Any Age.* As he reflected on this tough time in his life, he realized there was very little research for individuals to turn to as they navigated these difficult life events, despite the fact everybody unfortunately goes through them at some point in life.

What I imagine Bruce meant by this is that while there are a plethora of resources surrounding positive psychology, self-help, therapy, mindfulness, etc., Bruce craved more data around these traumatic events, the life transitions they cause, and how people cope with the change.

So, being a data-driven storyteller, he decided to interview hundreds of people living across all fifty states who had been through a recent major life change. These life changes included things like switching careers, shifting relationship status, losing a loved one or job, recovering from a health crisis, getting sober, etc. He then spent a year codifying the results to identify patterns, lessons learned, and common threads among these individuals.

As he dug into the data from his interviews, he found that we all go through a "disrupter" every twelve to eighteen months. Examples of what he defines as a "disrupter" are getting in an accident, changing jobs, moving, or even getting married.[28] I don't know about you, but I consider any of these events to be stress inducing and capable of making me think, "What just happened?" or "Am I sure I know what I'm doing?"

Importantly, "disrupters" are not all inherently negative life events. From the list, you can see some of the items listed are opportunities or even joyous events. Despite the positive outcomes, these occasions can also be stress-inducing times in our lives that cause turbulence.

And that's perfectly okay! Because, according to the data, these disrupters (positive and negative) are minor blips in the grand scheme of things that we are fairly good at managing.

The real problem arises with what Bruce calls "life quakes." These are massive changes in life that come with "aftershocks" for years, more specifically four to five years. These are what I affectionately call "Oh Shit Moments."

Bruce's data shows that we will go through a life quake three to five times in life, meaning we will spend twelve to

---

28   It seems to me marriage would be larger than just a "disruptor," as it's supposed to entail a lifelong change. That being said, we could argue about how to code each life event until we are blue in the face, so let's stick with Bruce's definitions for our purposes.

twenty-five years of our lives in transitions dealing with the "aftershocks" of these events.[29] That statistic is insane and terrifyingly sobering.

These life quakes are truly life-jarring and lead to a life transition in some way. Examples of life quakes from Bruce's data are death of a loved one, becoming seriously ill, going bankrupt, enduring a divorce, etc.

Needless to say, my father's two-year battle with cancer and eventual death was a life quake in my life that led to me quitting my job, earning my MBA, and writing this book! All the while, I was also going through a personal transformation that led to reflecting on what matters to me in life and striving to more consistently make decisions that best align with those priorities.

While I wish I could be writing a book about ways to avoid life quakes, or "Oh Shit Moments," the unfortunate truth is these life-altering moments are just as much a part of life as eating and breathing. They say nothing in life is certain

---

29 Bruce's research showed 80 percent of individuals use a ritual of some kind to signal to themselves that the traumatic event is in the past. In his interview on NPR, he shared, "They sang, they danced, they had memorial services, they got tattoos, they jumped out of airplanes; something to say to themselves and to others the past is over and I'm now heading in a new direction."

Additionally, Bruce found in the midst of the transition process, individuals commonly had two steps to help them move on in life. 1) They eliminated some aspect of their lives (drinking too much, working too hard, being too people pleasing, etc.) 2) They unleashed their creativity, be that song, dance, or the written word (hey, that's me with this book). Bruce shared, "Creativity helps us create ourselves anew."

but death and taxes. Perhaps they should include "Oh Shit Moments" to that list?

Okay, so now that my book has turned completely depressing and morbid, let's reframe this a bit.

While I can't help you completely avoid "Oh Shit Moments," I can help you be better prepared to deal with them whenever they do rear their ugly heads in your life. The point of Redefining Success for yourself now is so you can take the time to reflect on what matters to you and thoughtfully position yourself to live your life in alignment with your priorities.

That way, when something in life comes to wallop you, you are well-positioned to deal with the terribleness because you already have set yourself up for personal success.

Perhaps now you're thinking, "Okay, maybe I do buy into this whole idea of yours. But figuring out what I truly want and aligning my life around those priorities sounds terrifying and incredibly difficult."

Well, I won't sugarcoat it—of course it is! But you're not alone in feeling that way. This is a tough journey that even Olympians struggle with. And that's saying something because they are literally the best in the world at what they do.

In a conversation with Apolo Anton Ohno, the most decorated US Winter Olympian in US history with eight Olympic medals in short-track speed skating, he shared, "Pivoting in life and reinvention is really hard. All of us have our self-perceived...identities associated with what we do and who we are; and those are somehow intrinsically tied. So, as someone who didn't care about anything outside of the Olympic realm for fifteen years, I didn't know anything about what I was good at, what I was interested in, what I wanted to do next, and what my life purpose and true north was. It took a lot of self-discovery, self-realization, and self-work."[30]

In the discussion with Apolo, he shared the story of how he pivoted after retiring as an Olympian at the ripe age of twenty-eight. Let me say that again—he retired at the age of twenty-eight!

Take a second to imagine that. From the moment he won his first speed skating championship at the age of fourteen until the age of twenty-eight, everything in his life revolved around speed skating.[31] Everything from his diet, sleep routine, training regiment, and daily rituals were dictated by the sport. Then, at the age of twenty-eight, he found himself too old to compete in his profession any longer and had to retire.

What would you do if at twenty-eight years young you had to start anew?

Apolo shared, "From 2010, when I retired, until 2014, I was deeply afraid of getting stuck in this mental prison, that I

---

30 Let me address the elephant in the room as I just casually dropped the fact that I had the opportunity to be part of a conversation with Apolo Ohno. What a thrill! I vividly remember watching him crush the competition in the Olympics in 2002, 2006, and 2010.

31 Apolo won his first world championship in speed skating at the age of fourteen after only six months of training. Talk about being a natural at the sport!

was tied to that identity. At some point...all of us have to come to terms with those emotions. That means doing the thing that's the most important and most difficult in my view, which is looking in the mirror and having that radical, transparent conversation with yourself. And if you can't have it with yourself, find someone who you truly love who has the best interests for you...

"But I believe such a huge part of us growing as humans is accepting who we see in the mirror—in all of our flaws, inconsistencies, and 'less thans.' Only then can we start to move the needle forward and say, 'Alright, that's who I was and this is who I believe I can and will be, and it's going to be a long, arduous process of transformation.'"

Apolo's four-year transition just so happens to align perfectly with Bruce's research that life quakes and their associated aftershocks can take four to five years to overcome. Isn't it nice when things work out like that?

During this four-year stretch, Apolo revealed he did the only thing he knew how to do: "I moved as fast as I could." Except this time, it didn't mean skating around an ice rink, but trying anything and everything to jumpstart the next chapter of his life.

At one point, it almost seemed like he literally ran away from the problem, "spending a lot more time in Asia, pursuing these very nondescript businesses I had no experience doing." Needless to say, just like us mere non-Olympians, his transition was extremely hard and did not prove to be very fruitful at the start.

But by continuously trying new things and admittedly making "a ton of mistakes" along the way, Apolo has become a world-renowned speaker and author with a new calling in life. "My life's mission is to help people unlock their potential, to become the best version of themselves possible, so they can live, laugh, love, and produce their best work on earth." Sounds a bit like Redefining Success, doesn't it? Hey, that's my schtick!

He also continues to stay engaged with the US Olympics by sitting on the bid committee for the 2028 Summer Games, serving as an NBC sports analyst, and acting as a global ambassador to the Special Olympics and Winter Olympics. Of course, he also maintained his athletic prowess by winning Season Four of *Dancing with the Stars* and competing in an Ironman World Championship (Apolo Ohno, 2021).

By now, Part One of this book has hopefully made it clear to you time and time again that while your journey is unique, you're never alone. At this point, we've heard from the likes of an Olympic athlete, business tycoon, TV personality, whiskey distiller, marketing professional, college buddy, and many others—and all have struggled with Redefining Success for themselves.

That being said, by putting in the work, they have all reaped the incredible rewards of achieving greater alignment, happiness, and fulfillment in their lives by living with their priorities at the heart of every decision they made.

Now it's time to stop sitting on our butts and living vicariously through these wonderful folks. Okay, so maybe this is more of a mental process; feel free to remain seated, I suppose. But now it's time to act for ourselves so we can enjoy the same benefits as my examples from Part One!

In Part Two, I have distilled the key mindsets, tactics, research, and frameworks I have come across so you can Redefine Success for yourself.

Get ready to roll up your sleeves and get your hands dirty, we are about to enter the interactive portion of our journey together!

"We are all much more than what is on our business card or our LinkedIn profile. That's just what we do with the present moment. But that's not who we actually are."

–APOLO OHNO

KEY CHAPTER TAKEAWAYS

- We undergo a life "disrupter" every twelve to eighteen months in our lives. But good news! Despite the stress they cause, we are great at dealing with these "disrupters" when they take place.
- Throughout our lives, we will likely have to endure somewhere between three and five "Oh Shit Moments." Each "Oh Shit Moment" takes us an average of four to five years to recover from. But by Redefining Success for ourselves today, we are better prepared for these moments whenever they strike!
- When undergoing a life pivot, we need to remember to stay kind to ourselves because transitions are inherently

hard. But by giving ourselves time for self-discovery, self-realization, and self-work, we are able to define our priorities and align our lives to them accordingly for greater happiness and fulfillment.

PART 2

SCIENCE & STRATEGIES

CHAPTER 8

Vulnerability: Your Least Favorite Best Friend

Vulnerability Will Literally Save Your Life

"Vulnerability is kind of the core of shame and fear and our struggle for worthiness. But it's also the birthplace of joy, of creativity, of belonging, of love."

– BRENÉ BROWN

Buckle up—this will get bumpy.

No book about Redefining Success could be complete without bringing up the brilliance of Brené Brown, world-renowned expert in vulnerability, courage, shame, and empathy. The woman is an icon and responsible for one of the most watched TED talks of all time.

Seriously, if you haven't watched it yet, do yourself a favor and stop reading this book to watch her twenty-minute masterpiece titled, "The Power of Vulnerability." Go ahead…I'll wait for you to come back.

For those of you who may be unfamiliar, Brené is a professor at the University of Houston who has acquired a bit of a cult following due to her brilliance. She is the author of five *New York Times* bestselling books, has two of her own podcasts, and is frequently a guest on prominent podcasts like Adam Grant's *WorkLife*, *The Tim Ferriss Show*, and Oprah's *Super Soul Sunday*.

You know you've made it when you get invited to chat with Oprah!

In case you're not into podcasts, you also can catch Brené in the Netflix movie *Wine Country*, in which she plays herself. In the movie, Amy Poehler and Maya Rudolph's characters absolutely lose their minds when they meet Brené. Again, she's a bit of an icon at this point.

Now that we know Brené is *the* expert on vulnerability, what on earth does that mean for you and me? The answer is *everything*, because without vulnerability, we cannot be honest with ourselves or others and truly reflect to discover our desires, priorities, and goals in life. Without understanding and admitting those facets to ourselves, we have no chance of Redefining Success to achieve greater happiness, fulfillment, and alignment.

So, let's start with the obvious. What do I mean when I say vulnerability? Well, we can again turn to the trusted dictionary to give us a starting point. Merriam-Webster defines vulnerability as:

1. Capable of being physically or emotionally wounded.
2. Open to attack or damage.

I don't know about you, but based on those definitions, my self-preservation instincts tell me being vulnerable sounds like a terrible idea! If I were a robot, I'd be absolutely correct. The problem is we are human, and humans are incredibly complex.

In her 2010 TED talk, Brené Brown shared, "We live in a vulnerable world, and one of the ways we deal with it is we numb vulnerability. The problem is, and I learned this from the research, you cannot selectively numb emotion. You can't say, here's the bad stuff—here's vulnerability, here's grief, here's shame, here's fear, here's disappointment. I don't want to feel these. You can't numb those hard feelings without numbing the other effects or emotions. So, when we numb those [negative emotions], we numb joy. We numb gratitude. We numb happiness. And then we are miserable."

So, by limiting our vulnerability and negative emotions, we also self-limit our happiness and joy? I found this realization particularly devastating, as for the first decade of my professional career, I completely tried to avoid being vulnerable at work as I thought it would be unprofessional.

That's over forty hours a week, or over two thousand hours a year, of repressing my feelings!

Well, it turns out that not only did this limit my ability to feel positive emotions, but it also came with some seriously negative repercussions.

In 2011, researchers out of the University of Texas in Austin conducted an experiment in which subjects were forced to watch a disgusting scene from either the Monty Python's *The Meaning of Life* (overeating scene) or the 1996 film *Trainspotting* (toilet bowl scene). Participants were instructed either to react naturally or to "show no facial reactions whatsoever and to neutralize their innermost feelings" (Vohs et al., 2011).

Both sets of participants were then tasked with playing a game that helps to assess aggression. The participants who were forced to repress their emotions "let loose their urges and behaved aggressively."

What's fascinating to me is that each of us has a finite amount of self-regulatory capacity and once that capacity is depleted, we no longer can inhibit urges on a broader scale. In this instance, by having to repress emotions while watching a film, the study participants acted more aggressively in a game meant to measure aggression.

But studies have shown this self-regulation depletion can not only affect your emotions and mindset, but also cause you to cave more easily when it comes to your other vices, such as eating fatty or sugary foods, deciding to enjoy a smoke (if you were a former smoker), or consuming alcohol (Wagner, 2013).

Essentially, anything that requires self-regulation can be thought of as being in one big bundle, and once our self-regulation limit is reached, the floodgates open across the board. This helps explain why when you have a stressful day at work that makes you repress negative emotions in hopes of maintaining your professionalism, you're more likely to skip the gym, buy takeout, or partake in an alcoholic beverage—all things that require self-regulation to avoid.

I don't know about you, but at this stage of my research, my mind was blown. Who knew the consequences of repressing your vulnerability and negative emotions could be so profound? Well, luckily, now we both do.

So now that we know that being vulnerable and expressing our emotions, even the negative ones, are important for our wellbeing, the next logical question is how do we go about being more vulnerable? From my research, I see two stages of vulnerability: self-vulnerability and vulnerability with others.

1) SELF-VULNERABILITY

Being vulnerable with yourself often means listening to your inner voice or gut (metaphorically, that is, although if you're hungry, you should go grab a snack, too, I suppose). This could mean allowing yourself to daydream about the things that truly make you happy or simply asking yourself, "Why?" Why do I want to skip the gym today? Why am I feeling unhappy? Why am I dreading going to work? Why can't I stop thinking about my silly little side project?

The problem is, oftentimes, when you turn inward and begin to reflect, you will come across a problem or issue you are unsure how to address.

One tactic I have found incredibly useful in these situations is the Five Whys Technique, originally developed by Saki-chi Toyoda, the founder of Toyota Industries Corporation.[32] As straightforward as it seems, this framework states that when a problem arises, you can come to the root cause of the problem by asking a follow-up "why" question no more than five times (ASQ, 2021).

While this framework is extensively used in business (I learned about it in business school from a former McKinsey & Company partner), I personally have found this technique immensely useful when trying to grapple with my own personal thoughts and vulnerabilities.

In an effort to "practice what I preach," let me be vulnerable with you and share a personal example to illustrate how to use the Five Whys Technique.

To set the stage, after my father passed in 2018, I continued to work at my job, but was struggling mentally and emotionally. Despite seeing a grief therapist for months, I found myself worsening with time. For whatever reason, I was extremely hesitant to take a break, give myself the necessary time and space to process everything I had been through, and reevaluate my life.

---

32 The reason why the company is called "Toyota" as opposed to "Toyoda" after the founder's name is people thought it sounded better. Additionally, eight is a lucky number in Japan. By adjusting the name to "Toyota," it meant the name could be written in Japanese with eight strokes of the pen. With this in mind, the name was chosen in hopes that not only the company, but also Japan would prosper (Toyota, 2021).

This continued until April of 2019, when I finally was able to understand the root cause of my hesitation:

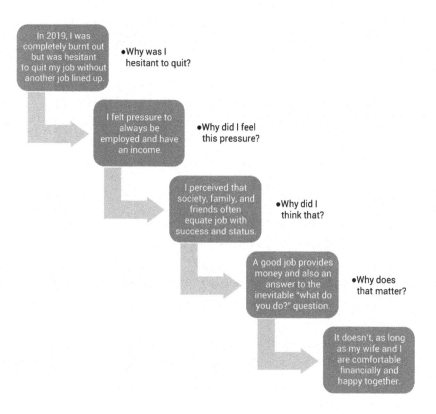

Admittedly, this self-reflection was a lot sloppier when I performed it in 2019, as I had not discovered the Five Whys Technique yet and was grappling with a tidal wave of emotion. Funny how logic can elude us sometimes when we need it most. However, through reflection, I eventually made it through this thought process.

In the end, the root cause of my hesitation to quit my job and take a break was being nervous about the financial ramifications being unemployed would have on my wife and me. So, to solve this pressure meant performing some careful financial forecasting and budgeting to understand what moving to one source of income would mean for our family.

For the record, I fully understand how fortunate I am to have my wife on my team. She absolutely saved the day by encouraging me to hit the metaphorical pause button on life to learn, reflect, reassess priorities, and rediscover my passions. Oh, and she agreed to be my sugar mama while I did all of this. What a deal!

That said, I also had to grapple with my fear of what others would think, which I addressed by "being productive" and becoming a fulltime MBA student. Now in hindsight, I'm very happy I chose to pursue my MBA, as it broadened my thinking and opened many doors.

But my reasons for doing so in 2019 were not ideal. While I knew an MBA would be useful in my future endeavors and was something I wanted to pursue eventually anyhow, my decision for pursuing it in 2019 was to have something impressive to say when someone asked me, "What do you do?"

Not a great reason, but to be fair, I never said I was perfect. Far from it!

Now, through my self-reflection, research, interviews, lessons, and writing this book, I've come to realize I must do my best to disregard what others may or may not think about my actions.

By no means is this easy. In fact, I still struggle with this mightily. But I am getting better at focusing my decisions on the things that matter to me. Ultimately, Terry McDougall (executive and career coach from Chapter Three) says it best: "You don't have any business knowing what other people think of you."

By being truly vulnerable with yourself, accepting your own thoughts and feelings, and asking yourself probing questions to understand the root cause of your problems, you will be ready to start brainstorming solutions and tangible next steps to better align your life around your priorities.

But inevitably, you will likely need your support network to help make these changes come to fruition. This brings us to step two of vulnerability.

2) VULNERABILITY WITH OTHERS

"Vulnerability is not winning or losing; it's having the courage to show up and be seen when we have no control over the outcome. Vulnerability is not weakness; it's our greatest measure of courage."

– BRENÉ BROWN

Let's be honest, truly opening yourself up to others is terrifying.

Even if you're talking to a spouse, family member, or close friend, conversations in which you share your true self are daunting. That said, having uncomfortable, vulnerable conversations is part of our daily lives.

Whether that means asking for a pay raise from your boss, telling your parents you no longer want to become a doctor, telling a special someone you love them for the first time, talking about your sex life with your significant other, or simply telling your friend you really can't stand their new haircut (okay, maybe that is a lesser example), these conversations are nerve-wracking.

By being vulnerable, you're putting yourself out there. What's terrifying is you have no idea what the other person will do or say in return. What if the other person gets angry? What if they are ashamed? What if they hate your new idea? What if they don't love you back? What if it's a haircut they've dreamed about for years?

Right before you start the conversation, inevitably your heart starts beating a bit faster, you breathe heavier, your palms get sweaty, you start to feel jittery, and you likely feel a rush of second thoughts about why the hell you're even doing this—all physiological symptoms of stress and anxiety (Mayo Clinic, 2021).

Why on earth do we want to have more of these conversations?

Think back on some of the vulnerable conversations you've had in life and try to remember the outcomes. Odds are that even if the initial reaction was not what you had hoped for, the vulnerable conversation likely led to a more fruitful relationship based on trust, honesty, and respect. Individuals you open up to in this fashion are the ones who wind up becoming the closest contacts you have. These individuals you are vulnerable with form your deepest connections.

A 1997 study by Arthur Aron and his colleagues at Stony Brook University really highlighted the importance of vulnerability when forming close relationships. This ground-breaking study asked complete strangers to have a forty-five-minute conversation with one another and then reflect on how close they felt with their randomly assigned partner.

Pairs were split into two groups. Group One was instructed to have a shallow conversation with their partner and were provided prompts such as "What is your favorite TV show?" and "What is your favorite holiday?"

Meanwhile, Group Two was instructed to have a deeper, more vulnerable conversation with prompts such as "When is the last time you cried in front of someone?" and "What is the role of love in your life?" and my personal favorite, "Out of all of the people in your family, whose death would you find the most disturbing?"

Can you imagine having these kinds of discussions with a stranger?

Unsurprisingly, Group Two indicated they felt much closer with their randomly assigned partner by forming deeper bonds through being vulnerable with one another. What is surprising, though, is this feeling of connectedness led to many of the individuals in Group Two reportedly maintaining friendships even after the study ended.

In a longer version of the same study, two participants from Group Two formed such a strong connection from this vulnerable discussion together that they wound up getting engaged a few months after the study (Simmons, 2014)!

So, if individuals reportedly feel closer and even get engaged simply by being vulnerable with a complete stranger, imagine what happens when you open up with your close friends and family.

Maybe now you believe me when I say vulnerability leads to closer relationships, but perhaps you're thinking to yourself, "Who cares? I don't want closer relationships if it means having to be more vulnerable with others."

Well, what if I told you your life literally depends on your ability to be vulnerable and form close relationships with others?

Scientists at Harvard University have proven the importance of close relationships in our lives by running an observational study for nearly eighty years. This study, which began back in 1938, tracked 724 participants throughout their lives. Participants came from two cohorts: Harvard University students and kids from Boston's poorest neighborhoods (Mineo, 2017).[33]

The study included surveys, medical exams, and interviews of each participant every two years. Additionally, the researchers interviewed parents and spouses to better understand the study participants' lifestyles and relationships. Lastly, the researchers also taped conversations between the subjects and their spouses to better gauge their connectedness.

---

33   Fun fact: John F. Kennedy—yes, JFK, the thirty-fifth president of the USA—was a part of the Harvard cohort!

In his 2015 TED talk describing the study results, Robert Waldinger, director of this landmark study, shared the key finding of this research was that "good relationships keep us happier and healthier. It's not just the number of friends you have and it's not whether or not you're in a committed relationship, but it's the quality of your close relationships that matters.

"When we gathered together everything we knew about [the participants] at age fifty, it wasn't their middle-age cholesterol levels that predicted how they were going to grow old. It was how satisfied they were in their relationships. The people who were the most satisfied in their relationships at age fifty were the healthiest at age eighty."

So, despite how scary it may seem, being vulnerable with others is vital to forming close connections and these meaningful relationships are the best predictor for our long-term happiness and health.

From this information, I think it's safe to say that vulnerability, no matter how scary and uncomfortable it makes us feel, is no longer optional in our lives. Vulnerability is required in order to truly understand our priorities, feelings, and goals in life so we can Redefine Success for ourselves while also forming deep connections with those we care about.

I don't know about you, but vulnerability has quickly become my least favorite new best friend.

Each and every person from Part One of this book managed to Redefine Success for themselves by embracing vulnerability. Arianna Huffington had the unfortunate experience of feeling physically vulnerable due to a health event that resulted from a misbalance in her life. She then used that wakeup call to be vulnerable with herself and reflect on how to maintain her business prowess in a healthier way.

Matthew Berry leveraged therapy to be vulnerable with himself and accept his true reality—that despite his Hollywood lifestyle, he was unhappy. He then expressed his vulnerability with his friends and family by sharing this truth and being pleasantly surprised by the acceptance he received.

Yanik Silver acknowledged his true feelings that despite his marketing accomplishments, he aspired for greater legacy and impact in his life. He shared these thoughts with his wife and began a more austere lifestyle to make a pivot in life possible, course-correcting through constant conversation with his partner until he found his true calling.

I myself have also attempted to become more vulnerable within my own life. I push myself to share my true thoughts and my full self with others, as opposed to my old style of compartmentalizing my life depending on my environment.

Like the others in Part One, this first required better understanding my true self through self-reflection and honesty—amazing how it's possible to be dishonest with yourself!

Second, it involved trusting those around me to accept my whole self—not just the good parts, the professional parts, or the secure parts, but also my imperfections, my personal self, and my insecurities. It's been a struggle, but it has allowed me to flourish into a new version of myself. And I won't lie, I really like this vulnerable "new me."

KEY CHAPTER TAKEAWAYS

- It is not possible to selectively numb negative emotions. If you choose to repress negative emotions, you will also be limiting your ability to feel positive emotions such as joy and happiness.
- We have a limited amount of self-regulatory capacity that is responsible for our ability to hide our emotions and control our urges. When we choose to repress our feelings, our ability to self-regulate dwindles across the board and increases the likelihood that we will give in to our vices.
- When you are struggling to identify the root cause of a problem, the Five Whys Technique can be a useful tool in understanding why you feel the way you do. It also happens to be great at identifying the root cause of a business problem.
- On a personal level, vulnerability allows for better self-awareness, reflection, and understanding of our true values and priorities in life. Vulnerability also is the key to forming close relationships, which are the best predictor for a happier, longer, and healthier life.

VULNERABILITY IN PRACTICE

Section 1 – Personal Vulnerability Exercises

Answer the following questions:
- How are you feeling about your life?
- What makes you upset?

- What makes you happy?
- What keeps you up at night?
- What gets you out of bed in the morning?
- What do you dread?
- What do you most look forward to?
- Are you living your best life?
- Are you proud of the person you've become?
- What would you do if fear was not a factor?
- What would you do if you could not fail?
- What are you most grateful for?
- What causes you stress in your life?
- Who are you most jealous of and why?

Once you have answered one or more of these questions, attempt the Five Whys Technique to identify the root cause (positive or negative) for any of your answers.

Section 2 – Vulnerability with Others Exercises

- **Practice making eye contact** – So often we avoid eye contact, as it can feel too emotional, raw, or awkward. When having conversations with individuals in your life, focus on maintaining eye contact. While this can feel uncomfortable, this demonstrates active listening and helps to communicate "I care and I am listening."
- **Ask for help** – Many of us struggle to admit when we do not know or cannot do something, as it can feel humbling. We are all human! No one knows everything—no matter how much they pretend they do. Even if the person you ask for help can't, perhaps they know someone who can or simply will be able to act as a sounding board as you seek clarity.

- **Express what you really want** – This can be in the form of sharing your responses to any of the questions in the Section One exercises of this chapter or perhaps revealing something else that's been on your mind. By sharing what you really want, you also open the door for the other individual to be honest with you, which will help to forge a deeper connection.
- **Apologize, share your feelings, and show appreciation** – All three of these are wonderful ways to foster deeper connection. Odds are if you practice one of these tactics, the individual you are sharing with will feel like they can open up with you as well.

CHAPTER 8 WORKBOOK
TIME TO TRY IT!

PERSONAL VULNERABILITY IN PRACTICE

Instructions: Choose your favorite question from the personal vulnerability exercises.

Write the Question Here:

Write Your Answer Below:

FIVE WHYS TECHNIQUE IN PRACTICE

Instructions: After writing down the answer to your favorite question, perform the Five Whys Technique to determine the root cause for your answer.

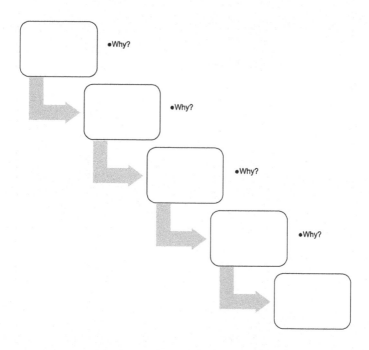

Challenge! Every day for the next week, choose a new question and write down your answers. Perform the Five Whys Technique each day.

VULNERABILITY WITH OTHERS IN PRACTICE

Instructions: Write down how you plan to practice being more vulnerable with someone within the next three days. Be specific! If possible, write down the who, what, where, when, why, and how of your plan.

Your Vulnerability Plan:

Who:

What:

Where:

When:

Why:

How:

Reflection/Results: After you carry out your vulnerability plan, answer the following questions:

How did your interaction make you feel?

What were the outcomes?

How did the other person respond?

Challenge! Make a vulnerability plan for yourself for every day of the next week! Each day, reflect and write down how your vulnerability exercises went, what the outcomes were, and how they made you feel.

Week-Long Vulnerability Plan

Reflection/Results: After you carry out your vulnerability plan, answer the following questions:

How did your interactions make you feel?

What were the outcomes?

How did the other people respond?

What made some interactions more effective or meaningful than others?

CHAPTER 9

Gratitude: The Antidote to Toxic Comparisons

Increasing Our Social Interactions While
Practicing Gratitude Generates Happiness

Imagine you're riding on a train. You find a seat and enjoy the luxury of not having anyone sitting next to you. Peace, tranquility, personal space, and a moment to yourself. How lovely does that sound?

As the train arrives at the next station and other riders hop on, you hear someone ask you the dreaded four-word question, "Is anyone sitting there?" as they point to the seat next to you.

What runs through your brain at that moment?

I don't know about you, but as I politely say, "Nope, it's all yours," a million thoughts run through my head.

Things like:

- Seriously? You couldn't have picked any other seat?
- Ugh, so much for relaxing.
- Let the battle for the shared armrest begin!

Maybe I'm more of an introvert than you are, but I would venture to guess that even if these kinds of thoughts don't flood your brain, the likelihood is you plan to finish this train ride without talking to this stranger at all. Chances are you not only feel sitting in silence is the socially acceptable thing to do, but you would also simply enjoy the quiet time better than interacting with a random person.

What if I told you our instincts in this scenario are wrong? If we want to maximize our happiness during that train ride, silence is not golden.

Nicholas Epley and Juliana Schroeder, researchers at the University of Chicago Booth School of Business, performed an experiment in 2014 in which they instructed commuters on a train to either "connect with a stranger near them, remain disconnected, or commute as normal."

Prior to the experiment, participants predicted they would have a more positive experience when they were not forced to interact with anyone and were simply able to ride in solitude. But as you can guess from my setup, after the train ride was over, participants reported a more positive experience when they interacted with someone.

I know what you're thinking: "This may be true for extroverts, but certainly not for introverts." Wrongo. Regardless of whether participants were self-proclaimed extroverts or introverts, the results were the same.

In case you think this is a weird train phenomenon, this study was repeated on buses, in waiting rooms, and even on the London Tube.[34]

In an excerpt for the BBC, Dr. Epley shared, "These brief connections with strangers are not likely to turn a life of misery into one of bliss. However, they can change unpleasant moments, like the grind of a daily commute, into something more pleasant" (Christian, 2019).

As we already learned in Chapter Three, the key to happiness lies in enjoying the journey, not the destination. In this case, that cliché applies both figuratively and literally.

From his 2014 publication, Dr. Epley went on to explain, "Humans are among the most social species on the planet, with brains uniquely adapted for living in large groups. Feeling

---

34 The London Tube, also known as the London Underground, is the train system within London, England. The Tube was first constructed in 1863 between Bishop's Road (Paddington) and Farringdon Street. At this time, the railways were just below surface level and were used by steam-powered trains that pulled along wooden carriages. Nearly forty thousand people used the new railway on the day it opened.

Fast forward to 1890, when technology then allowed for much deeper railways to be built under the city. Deep, circular tunnels were dug under the city and transitioned to electric trains. Upon opening these new lines, the city advertised the improved offering as the "Central London (Tube) Railway" and was referred to by residents as the "twopenny tube" due to the cost to ride the new train. This was eventually shortened to "the Tube" by locals over the years (Kingsley, 2020).

socially connected increases happiness and health, whereas feeling disconnected is depressing and unhealthy."

So, in light of this information, I urge you to push yourself out of your comfort zone and socialize more often. However, I also want to caution you about one of the unfortunate tendencies that can quickly wipe out all of the valuable gains we enjoy when we are social: comparing ourselves to others.

WHEN YOU CATCH YOURSELF COMPARING YOURSELF TO OTHERS, REMEMBER, YOUR PATH IS YOURS AND YOURS ALONE

"Comparison is the thief of joy."

— THEODORE ROOSEVELT

Would you rather earn 50,000 dollars a year or 100,000 dollars a year?

That seems like a dumb question, right?

Well, what if I told you 52 percent of Harvard University students responded by saying they'd prefer to make 50,000 dollars a year? Does that change your answer at all? I certainly hope not! Remember what your mother always told you about not jumping off a bridge just because your friends did?

Okay, so what's the catch? Either Harvard students are not as smart as we all thought or the question was actually more complicated than I made it out to be. In reality, the real options presented to the 159 Harvard University students in this 1998 research study by Drs. Solnick and Hemenway were the following:

Circle either A or B, or if undecided, both A and B:

- *Note prices are what they are currently and prices (the purchasing power of money) are the same in States A and B.*
  - *A) Your current yearly income is 50,000 dollars; others earn 25,000 dollars.*
  - *B) Your current yearly income is 100,000 dollars; others earn 200,000 dollars.*

Yes, 52 percent of the Harvard students chose Option A—to earn less money as long as it meant they made more than other people.[35] So much for the old expression: "a rising tide lifts all ships."

While I found these results staggering, I thought to myself, "Okay, perhaps these results are just skewed because these are students without the benefit of 'real-world' experience. After all, these kids have literally been in competition with their peers for their entire lives in order to get into Harvard. How could they know any better? Surely, individuals a bit more

---

35 This survey actually included twelve similar questions ranging from items like your own attractiveness, IQ level, education amount, vacation amount, your children's attributes, etc. Shockingly, the question that led to the highest positional answer (meaning respondents preferred to have less of an absolute score as long as it meant having more relatively to others) was when respondents were asked:
- *A: Your child's attractiveness is six; others average four.*
- *B: Your child's attractiveness is eight; others average ten.*
80 percent of students and 46 percent of faculty/staff chose Option A in this scenario!

removed from school wouldn't be so concerned with their relative position to others and would prefer to make more money."

Not so much. The same survey was administered to seventy-nine Harvard University faculty and staff in the study and a whopping 35 percent of these individuals still chose Option A. How could anyone willingly choose to make so much less just to one-up the competition?

This is the unfortunate truth of our world. No matter how much we make, have, or accomplish, we frequently want to compare our achievements and circumstances to others to make sure we are doing better than they are.

That being said, this was back in 1998, so perhaps things have gotten better and folks no longer care to compare? I would actually argue, in fact, things have gotten even worse.

Today's digital age is filled with a seemingly endless list of social media platforms that keep us up to date on everything everyone is doing all the time. It's great! Or is it?

You have LinkedIn telling you to congratulate your former colleague for recently becoming a vice president. Facebook notifications with all of the new pictures of your friends showing just how perfect their vacation, engagement, kids, and families are. Friends Snapping and Instagramming pictures of decadent foods, insane parties, and every single fun moment you are missing.

Inevitably, that's when the dreaded four-letter acronym kicks in: FOMO (or "fear of missing out," in case you forgot).

Remember Patrick McGinnis, the inventor of FOMO? We met him in Chapter Three.

There are countless studies illustrating that increased social media usage is correlated with decreased sleep and higher levels of anxiety and depression. Some studies even take it a step further to correlate rising suicide rates in adolescents to social media usage. And despite it not being an official medical condition, FOMO is often cited in the research as a cause (Mir, Nova, and Seymour, 2021).

People are constantly broadcasting the best parts of their lives hoping to get one more "like" or one more follower than yesterday. It's a product of the digital age we live in. What's even crazier, though, is society incentivizes this behavior.

If somehow you manage to entertain the world enough with your controversial Tweets, posh Instagram pictures, or new TikTok dance, the world will literally pay you for it by making you a social influencer, simply encouraging you to partake in these activities even more.

Celebrities of the world can attract up to 300,000 dollars for a social media post that promotes a given product! While that astronomical level is reserved for a select few, even individuals with less than one thousand followers can make some cash on the side for sharing posts on social media. The better content you generate, the more followers you attract, which leads to more money in your bank account. It's a vicious reward cycle. Get to one hundred thousand followers and earn 700 to 900 dollars per photo. Reach the five-hundred-thousand-follower mark and you can command about 2,000 to 3,000 dollars per sponsored photo posted (Geyser, 2021).

The world has become so starved for constant content and addicted to stimulus that there are dogs that make more money than me by being "influencers" on a whole host of social media platforms. If dogs throughout history have taught us anything, it's even the smallest rewards can reinforce almost any behavior, good or bad—and that includes drooling. Thanks, Pavlov!

In 2018, the first prospective study across multiple social media platforms found "limiting social media usage does have a direct and positive impact on subjective wellbeing over time, especially with respect to decreasing loneliness and depression" (Hunt et al., 2018).

The problem is that after our initial "like" or "comment" showing our support, our thoughts often turn inward. This culture of comparison is an unfortunate byproduct of the constant stream of life updates.

A 2008 study published in the *Journal of Experimental Social Psychology* by Drs. Summerville and Roese found 12 percent of our thoughts are comparative in nature, and comparison almost never ends well.

While comparison can create motivation for improvement, recent studies have found people who regularly compare themselves to others have feelings of deep dissatisfaction, guilt, or remorse which can even lead to destructive behaviors (Psychology Today, 2021).

We've all been there. We're scrolling endlessly through social media posts when thoughts like these pop into our head:

- "She's seeing the northern lights while I'm sitting on my couch eating potato chips and watching *The Office* reruns. Should I be doing more with my life?" Let's be honest, one could argue that the answer is likely no in this particular case because *The Office* is fantastic!
- "How can that guy be more accomplished than me when he was such an underachiever in high school? Didn't I once see him pass out from sniffing glue? Where did I go wrong?"
- "Does she ever stop doing volunteer work? Who does she think she is, Mother Teresa? Ugh, I should do more volunteer work and be a better person."
- "What the hell am I doing with my life?"

It's all so negative.

But what's baffling to me is that no one is spared from these inner thoughts. Even those at the top of their industry feel this way from time to time.

Matthew Berry, Emmy Award winner and the face of fantasy football we met in Chapter One, shared, "There's always somebody who, real or imagined, is more successful than you. Who has more friends, or more money, or is better looking, or healthier, or well-respected, or whatever it is.

"I don't care how famous you are, how successful you are, how brilliant you are, [or how] top of the world you are, there's always somebody. It's a very real thing, FOMO, and

I'm actually going through it now too. I ask myself why I did that two years ago. I should have seen this trend or I should have seen that.

"And then there's part of me that's like, 'Listen, Berry. You saw the fantasy football rise and you rode that...and have done very well in a lot of areas because of that. Why don't you just sit back, enjoy your life, and pat yourself on the back?'

"[...] But it's hard to turn off. You have to remind yourself life isn't a race; it's a journey and everyone's journey and path is different. Your path isn't better or worse than anyone else's. It's just yours."

What a beautiful sentiment.

By now you're probably thinking, "Social media is the worst. All it does is make me want to compare myself to others and the research behind comparisons is terrifying. Let's burn social media at the stake!"

Not so fast, though! I'm not advocating for you to completely abandon technology and go live in a cabin. Social media provides fantastic opportunities to remain connected with friends, family, and peers across the globe with the click of a button or swipe of a phone.

These connection points help us maintain and build relation-ships—and we just learned that being social and maintain-ing quality relationships are vital to our lives and wellbeing. Just like anything in life (excluding bacon), it's all about moderation and learning how to process the wealth of information at your fingertips without feelings of resentment, jealousy, or inadequacy.

In fact, the same 2018 study that sounded so damning regarding social media actually found limiting our social media usage to thirty minutes a day seemed to be the sweet spot. Additionally, the researchers highlighted improving our own self-monitoring and awareness of use would likely be beneficial. It's about catching ourselves when we stop celebrating others' successes and instead turn inwards to compare our lives to theirs.

While this study does provide a nice starting point as guidance, I would argue that understanding your own personal sweet spot is highly reliant on you. Things like age, socioeconomic status, introvert vs. extrovert, cultural norms, religion, personality, interests, upbringing, family life, and a whole host of other factors all feed into the metaphorical equation that determines how much and what forms of social media each one of us can consume before hitting our threshold.

Unfortunately, it seems the ideal balance is achieved through experimentation and self-reflection. After spending some time scrolling through your favorite social media site, ask yourself:

- How do I feel?
- Was there content that made me feel more negative about myself?
- When I saw someone else's positive news, did I turn inward and feel jealous, insecure, or less accomplished?

In an episode of the *Entrepreneurs on Fire* podcast with John Lee Dumas, John shared a story of a beautiful picture he and his wife took atop a cliff overlooking the ocean. It was an absolutely majestic view. He shared the picture on social media and received a plethora of likes and positive feedback like, "Oh my god, I would give everything to be there!"

It turns out that picturesque scene was actually a terrible experience! It was so cold, wet, and windy they had to scrap their plans and leave immediately. John ended the story with, "Sometimes a pretty picture is a miserable experience." While this may be a silly example, it is a perfect metaphor for the lens through which we typically view each social media post.

On a more macro level, we need to remember that for every amazing picture or story posted, there is more than meets the eye and associated tradeoffs to consider.

For instance, the amazingly accomplished business person at times envies the stay-at-home parent for all of those precious moments they get to enjoy with their kids. Likewise, the stay-at-home parent sometimes desires the business person's career achievements and the associated perks that come from them.

The family person who enjoys a relaxing Saturday night at home at times yearns for the days of leaving the bar at 2:00 a.m. without a care in the world. Meanwhile, the bargoer may just be looking to find that special someone to curl up on a couch with for a quiet night at home.

It's the proverbial grass is greener on the other side mentality. As hard as it is, we all need to break that vicious cycle if we are to have any hopes of truly achieving happiness because, in reality, the grass is greener wherever you nurture it.

"Compare yourself to one person—you yesterday. If you are winning that comparison, you will be winning at life. Period. And you don't have to be winning that comparison every single day, because we all have down days. But more times than not, if you are winning that comparison, you will win."

—*JOHN LEE DUMAS*

GRATITUDE SAVES THE DAY!

So, we now know that to be happier, we need to be social and build connections. However, by being social, we are often tempted to compare ourselves to others, which makes us more anxious, unhappy, and depressed.

This sounds like we can't win no matter what we do!

However, there is a secret weapon to combat the comparison game we all like to play: gratitude.

Robert Emmons, professor of psychology at the University of California, Davis, is considered one of the world's leading experts on gratitude. He's the author of over two hundred peer-reviewed journal publications and has published three books on the topic of gratitude. It seems Dr. Emmons is just about as good a source as we can hope for when it comes to figuring out how gratitude can save the day.

So, let's see what Dr. Emmons has to say about gratitude. Through his work, Dr. Emmons argues there are two crucial elements that define gratitude:

- An affirmation of goodness. We affirm there are good things in the world, gifts and benefits we've received.
- A recognition the sources of this goodness are outside of ourselves. We acknowledge other people—or even higher powers, if you're of a spiritual mindset—gave us many gifts, big and small, to help us achieve the goodness in our lives (*Greater Good Magazine*, 2021).

We all have countless things to be grateful for, but our tendency is to focus on the things others have that we want rather than everything we already have.

If you recall from Chapter Three, we learned that oftentimes hedonic adaptation kicks in and we end up becoming used to the things we have in life, which in turn diminishes the positive feelings we have because of them. But what if we took the time to truly appreciate the things we have by practicing gratitude?

It turns out the research shows there are massive positive consequences to practicing gratitude. Even simple actions like sharing our gratitude with others or simply writing down the things we are grateful for can have great effects on our wellbeing. In 2020, Robert Emmons shared expressing gratitude allows us to:

- Celebrate the present
- Block toxic emotions like envy, resentment, regret, and depression

- Become more stress-resilient
- Strengthen our social ties and feelings of self-worth

Bullet point number two directly addresses the negative consequences of comparing ourselves to others. Isn't it nice when things work out like that?

Perhaps even more importantly from Dr. Emmons' work is the fact that by regularly practicing gratitude, we become more stress-resilient. As we learned in Chapter Seven from Bruce Feiler's work, we can expect to experience disruptive life events every twelve to eighteen months. By regularly practicing gratitude, we can be better equipped to handle the stress those disruptors cause us.

Additionally, Laurie Santos, Yale positive psychologist, shared the following about the effect gratitude has on our happiness during her 2020 interview on *Clear+Vivid with Alan Alda*: "Gratitude is another thing we know is super correlated with feeling happy. Happy people are counting their blessings. They're focused on the things that make them happy and they're really thankful for.

"But more importantly, they express it. They spontaneously express their gratitude to the people around them. And when you think about it, there's a lot of people in our life we're grateful for, but we often don't say it.

"And if you ask, 'Why don't you say it?' it's because it would feel weird. We predict awkwardness but actually, in practice, it feels really good, both for the person who's hearing the gratitude and for the person who's expressing it."

As I went through my own personal journey, I can tell you the power of gratitude is absolutely astounding. From my own firsthand experience of incorporating gratitude exercises and mindsets in my life, I can tell you the simple practice of focusing on the positive things you have has a profound way of reframing the events and circumstances of your own life.

I've shared a few of the seemingly simple gratitude exercises my wife and I have implemented in our lives below and cannot understate the positive effects that these have had on us. Perhaps the best part of all of the exercises is that they are *free* and take very little time or effort. So, no excuses to not try them out for yourself.

KEY CHAPTER TAKEAWAYS

- Trying to be more social, even with strangers, increases your happiness in the moment, regardless of whether you identify as an introvert or an extrovert.
- Nobody is immune to playing the comparison game from time to time—even those at the top of their respective fields do it! But comparing ourselves to others often leads to negative emotions such as deep dissatisfaction, guilt, or remorse. Be sure to take time to celebrate others without judging yourself or feeling inadequate.
- Studies have shown limiting social media usage can have a direct and positive impact on our wellbeing over time.
- Only compare yourself to one person—you from yesterday!
- Gratitude is like a superpower! Practicing gratitude increases our happiness, makes us more resilient to stress, blocks toxic emotions, and increases our feelings of self-worth. Practicing gratitude means you celebrate all you

have and appreciate the others who have helped you get to where you are today.

BEING MORE SOCIAL – IN PRACTICE

- Practice simply waving, smiling, or saying hello to individuals in your neighborhood or workplace. Such a simple touch can make individuals feel more welcome and brighten their day, along with your own!
- Reach out to someone from your past who you haven't spoken with in a while. Perhaps it's an old colleague or friend you regrettably lost contact with. If possible, try to set up some time to connect via phone, videocall, or in person to catch up.
- Invite someone from your office you don't know too well to have lunch or grab a coffee. Make it a goal to get to know one new colleague per week (or month). While you can certainly chat about work topics, I would encourage you to try and get to know more about that individual on a personal level. Questions to consider:
  - What do you like to do when you're not working?
  - What was your favorite vacation?
  - Have you read any good books or enjoyed any new shows lately?
- Stretch goal: Next time you are in a public situation in which you feel conversation is frowned upon (on an elevator, on a plane or train, in line, etc.), try striking up a conversation with someone around you. Be courteous and be sure to respect their boundaries and desires! While this may feel uncomfortable, Dr. Epley's research tells us that you and your newfound connection are both ultimately more likely to enjoy the time and feel happier.

EXPRESSING GRATITUDE – IN PRACTICE

- Daily Gratitude Exercise: Select a time each day to start a new gratitude routine. Every day, at your selected time, answer the following question: what are you thankful for today?
  - I would recommend you set a daily reminder in your calendar for the same time so you can get into the habit. Alternatively, add a sticky note to your bathroom mirror so you answer the question while you are getting ready to start or end your day.
- Keep a Good News Box or Gratitude Journal: My wife and I started a Good News Box in 2017 and haven't stopped. The below instructions can also be implemented with a gratitude journal instead.
  - Instructions: Designate a container (we used a box, but any container will do) and label it with "Good News." Keep the Good News Box in a prominent location in your home (kitchen or living room). Keep scratch paper and a writing utensil next to the box at all times. Anytime something good happens in your life, take a moment to write it down on a piece of paper and place it in the Good News Box. Alternatively, dedicate a specific time each week to reflect on all of the good things from the week and add any good news from the week to the box. Aim to add a minimum of five pieces of paper to the box each week.
  - At the end of every month, take time to open the box and read all of the pieces of paper you added for the month. Do not throw the pieces of paper away, but simply store them for the time being. This way, at the end of the year, you can review all of the good news from the entire year!

- Send Notes/Letters of Gratitude
  - Every week, send thank-you notes to three people in your life. These individuals can be friends, family, colleagues, or peers. The messages can be as short or long as you want, but be sure to express how grateful you are to have these people in your life and what specific impact they have had on you that you are thankful for.

CHAPTER 9 WORKBOOK
TIME TO TRY IT!

BEING MORE SOCIAL IN PRACTICE

Instructions: Write down how you plan to be more social with someone within the next three days. Be specific! If possible, write down the who, what, where, when, why, and how of your plan.

Your Being More Social Plan:

Who:

What:

Where:

When:

Why:

How:

Reflection & Results: After completing your being more social plan, answer the following questions:

How did your interaction make you feel?

What were the outcomes?

How did the other person respond?

Challenge! Make a social plan for the next month. Every week, aim to have at least one interaction with someone you've lost touch with or don't typically connect with in your office or neighborhood. Be sure to make time for Reflection & Results.

Month-Long Social Plan

Reflection & Results: After completing your being more social plan, answer the following questions:

How did your interactions make you feel?

What were the outcomes?

How did the other people respond?

What made some interactions more positive than others?

EXPRESSING GRATITUDE IN PRACTICE

Instructions: In order to kickstart your new gratitude routines, whether that be a daily gratitude exercise, Good News Box, or journal, it's time to get the ball rolling!

List three things you are grateful for today:

1)

2)

3)

List three people who you are grateful to have in your life below:

1)

2)

3)

Send each individual who you listed above a thank-you note expressing why you are grateful to have them in your life. A letter, e-mail, text, or handwritten note is perfectly acceptable. What's most important is you choose the mechanism you will do now.

Reflection & Results: How did each person respond to your note of gratitude?

1)

2)

3)

How do you feel after expressing your gratitude to these three individuals?

Challenge! Create a Good News Box or gratitude journal for yourself. Every day for the thirty days, add at least one thing you are grateful for to your box/journal. When one of your entries has to do with the actions or presence of someone else in your life, be sure to reach out to that person to let them know!

Prior to starting your month of gratitude, reflect on the following questions:

Do you have any predictions for what your gratitude entries will include?

How do you feel about your life?

Reflection & Results: After your thirty days of gratitude, review all of your gratitude entries and answer the following questions:

What trends do you notice in your gratitude entries for the last month? How do they compare to your prediction?

How do you feel about your life? How does that compare to your entry from thirty days ago?

CHAPTER 10

Passion and the Growth Mindset: Two Peas in a Pod

**The Growth Mindset Is Crucial to
Your Personal Development**

All too often we hear the advice to "follow your passions."
But what does that mean?

Throughout my interviews and research, I encountered a
kaleidoscope of thoughts surrounding passion which were
simultaneously enlightening and immensely confusing given
how inconsistent all of the ideas were.

In this book alone, we heard from Matthew Berry (the face
of fantasy football) who said, "If you chase happiness and
your passion, that's what I believe leads to success." We also
heard from David Perkins (High West founder), in which

he literally credited passion as the currency for his distillery when the bank account was running low.

Conversely, Yanik Silver (Maverick1000 founder) prefers words like "enthusiasm" and "inspiration" to passion, because passion alone is not enough—sustaining power is needed as well. Mike O'Donnell (college buddy turned barbeque mogul) said, "I don't necessarily think passion is a good reason to start a business. I think it's going to destroy your passion." And while not a story I highlighted in this book, the ever-entertaining Mark Cuban (billionaire, *Shark Tank* investor, and owner of the Dallas Mavericks) has even gone as far to say, "One of the great lies of life is [to] follow your passions." Ouch.

So naturally, I had to do more digging to see if I could wrap my head around what passion really is and how you can discover your own passions. In my quest to learn more, I found a plethora of perspectives on the subject that downright contradicted each other, just like my examples above.

How on earth do we make sense of it all? If passion is important, how do we find what we are passionate about? Do we develop our passions or are they something we're born with?

Well, lucky for you, I think I've found the answer to simplify the matter. It seems the varying viewpoints on passion boil down to two broader schools of thought: fixed mindset vs. growth mindset.

While there are many incredible researchers who have studied the growth mindset at length—notably it was Carol Dweck (Stanford University psychologist) who actually coined the term "growth mindset" through various publications and her book, *Mindset,* based on her work studying thousands of kids.

Dr. Dweck asserts that those individuals with a growth mindset feel our attributes can change over time as we work to better ourselves and learn. Alternatively, those with a fixed mindset believe we are born with certain attributes and simply need to harness them—in other words, our attributes are unchangeable.

While Dr. Dweck and her colleagues focused primarily on intelligence in their studies, the idea of having a fixed or growth mindset has since been expanded to aspects such as personality, willpower, shyness, passion, etc. And it's important to note that just because someone has a particular mindset about one of their attributes does not mean they necessarily have that same mindset about all of their attributes.

For example, a person may feel they were born with a certain amount of intelligence and no matter what they do, their intelligence will not change (fixed mindset). However, they may also feel they can work to improve their shyness over time by practicing public speaking to become more outgoing (growth mindset). It's highly reliant on the individual!

In her book, *Mindset,* published in 2006, Dr. Dweck emphasizes the power of beliefs and mindsets as "they strongly affect what we want and whether we succeed in getting it."

Interesting. It makes sense a mindset would affect our desires, but shouldn't ability be the ultimate driver of accomplishment? Apparently not—well, at least not entirely.

She went on to explain that those with a fixed mindset prefer tasks they know they are good at and tend to shy away from challenges. Meanwhile, those with a growth mindset see challenges and failure as opportunities for improvement and future preparedness.

Researchers at Michigan State University performed a fascinating study looking at the effects that having a fixed mindset or a growth mindset can have when individuals make a mistake or fail. In this 2011 study led by Dr. Jason Moser, subjects performed a Theories of Intelligence Scale (TIS) to first indicate whether they had a fixed or growth mindset coming into the study.[36] The subjects were then hooked up to brain monitors in order to measure event-related potentials (science speak for electrical signals in the brain) as they performed tasks and inevitably made mistakes.

The researchers found that those individuals who came into the study with a fixed mindset had little to no activity as they made mistakes in the exercises. These individuals did not engage with the errors or have a desire to learn from them, as they felt their intelligence was fixed.

---

36 The Theories of Intelligence Scale was developed by Dr. Dweck and her colleagues as a way to determine someone's belief about learning and intelligence (i.e., whether someone has a fixed or growth mindset). In this study, the researchers asked participants to complete a short assessment in which they had to score statements on a Likert-type scale (one = strongly disagree, six = strongly agree). An example of a provided statement is: "You have a certain amount of intelligence and you really cannot do much to change it." Based on the participants' responses, they were designated as either having a growth mindset (low score) or fixed mindset (high score) for the purposes of the experiment.

However, the subjects who came into the study with the growth mindset had their brains firing loads of electrical signals, indicating deep engagement as they attempted to learn, correct, and improve for the future.

It's no wonder Dr. Dweck argues that beliefs and mindsets "affect what we want and whether we succeed in getting it." A commitment to learning and personal growth is imperative if we are to continue improving ourselves and achieving our goals.

Now, you may be thinking, "Oh, great, it's all about how my brain sends electrical signals, so that must be genetic. I'm doomed." But not so fast! Advances in neuroimaging and psychology have allowed researchers to better understand the brain. The good news is the human brain is extremely malleable and adaptive, something neuroscientists call brain plasticity. All this means is through our experiences and practice, our neural networks can strengthen, grow new connections, and even become faster (Mindset Works, 2021).

What's even more encouraging is that through neuroimaging studies, it's been proven that our brain's ability to learn and adapt continues throughout our entire life (Fishbane, 2015). The old expression "you can't teach an old dog new tricks" has officially been debunked!

Effectively, we can learn and better ourselves through practice regardless of our age. So, anyone can train themselves to think more in the growth mindset over time.

Let's explore the ramifications of each mindset on passion.

FIXED MINDSET AND PASSION

When it comes to passion in particular, those with a fixed mindset feel we are born with our passions and simply need to discover them.

These individuals tend to think our passions are innate and that when we find and accept our passions, they will lead to unlimited motivation, making any endeavor involving our passion seemingly effortless. Hence the guidance: "follow your passions"!

Viewing passion with the lens of a fixed mindset tends to lead to less likelihood of trying new activities once you already have found what you perceive to be your true passion. Also, if you take up your passion and suddenly encounter problems or roadblocks, you are quick to think, "Perhaps this wasn't for me after all," and you will embark on a new journey to find your *true* passion since it should feel easy.

GROWTH MINDSET AND PASSION

Those with a growth mindset feel our passions develop over time. As we work and invest our time, money, and sweat into a given activity, our enjoyment and appreciation for it will grow until it eventually becomes a passion. Marissa Fernandez (executive coach from Chapter Four) shared this perspective of passion during our interview together and brilliantly said, "Passion equals curiosity plus effort."

Similar to a fixed mindset, actually finding our passion is trial and error. The difference is that with a fixed mindset, you will know it's your passion very quickly, while with a growth mindset, it may take some time to grow on you, like a fungus! *Twice in the same book; doesn't this guy have different expressions?*

Perhaps more importantly, with a growth mindset, having a strong interest in one area does not preclude you from trying and developing passions in other areas.

Additionally, because passions need to be developed, there is greater tolerance when the passion becomes frustrating or difficult. Just like my experience with the pesky cello when I was in fourth grade, anything we practice will simply get easier over time (although I'm pretty sure it still sounded like a dying cat when I played. Sorry, Mom!)

GROWTH MINDSET EXPANDED

"Your level of success will rarely exceed your level of personal development, because success is something you attract by the person you become."

– JIM ROHN (ELROD, 2012)

All of my stories in Part One are stellar examples of how the growth mindset can drastically improve your own personal journey. To revisit one example specifically, though, Mike O'Donnell has leveraged a growth mindset consistently throughout his life.

Whether it was accepting an unpaid internship to maximize learning potential, attending a random conference in Houston to hear more about search engine optimization, or accepting an invitation to a seemingly random retreat in Lithuania, each decision involved a conscious choice to prioritize personal growth and learning over immediate financial gains or perceived success. Each decision Mike made ultimately led to long-term growth and accomplishments for him.

While Mike's examples may not be easy to replicate given the circumstances, the point is to remain curious and pursue growth opportunities. Simple activities such as listening to enlightening podcasts, reading about personal development (hey, you're doing that with this book!), and seeking out free educational resources to expand your horizons on new topics are very tangible steps anyone can take to embody the growth mindset.

Learning and growth have always been central pillars of my identity thanks in large part to my parents. My mom was a teacher for over twenty-five years, both in Spain and the United States. The woman was born to teach—talk about passion! To this day, she still lights up any time she has the chance to make a positive impact on a young mind. She has the unique blend of patience, dedication, intelligence, and love that makes her truly great at her profession. She is to teaching what Wayne Gretzky is to hockey. I'm not biased or anything, though…

I was fortunate enough to grow up with this incredible teacher in my house. From the furthest I can remember, she would work with me on every subject. While so many of my elementary school counterparts regressed in the summer due to the lack of school, structure, and subject reinforcement, I would continue to improve and learn due to constant lessons at home. She did this every year despite my incessant complaining that it was the summer and I just wanted to go play. I was a pain…thank you, Mom!

On the other side, my dad was also a huge proponent of learning and growth. You'll hear more about him in the Conclusion, but he had an engineering degree and an MBA. But more than that, he was constantly trying to learn and improve himself. His tagline in life was: "Learn Something!" He said this so often that one year for his birthday, I even photoshopped his face on to the infamous Uncle Sam picture and replaced the "I Want You" slogan with "Learn Something."

This small glimpse into my upbringing helps explain my commitment to learning and growth. How else can you explain my decision to finish a bachelor's and not one, but two master's degrees before the age of thirty-two?

Some say I'm a glutton for punishment—in fact, I say this, too, at times—but in reality, it's because learning has been engrained into my soul as a key tenet of life.

LEARNING AND GROWTH—PROFESSIONAL, PERSONAL, BOTH?

No matter what you decide to do in life or how unbelievably accomplished you might be, learning and growth are important professionally. After all, the world is an incredibly competitive place.

Whether you are an employee at a conglomerate, part of a small start-up, entrepreneur, medical professional, lawyer, teacher, student, service worker, or any other profession, the growth mindset will help you achieve your goals, remain ahead of the competition, and take tangible steps toward your desired career progression.

More broadly, though, I argue the growth mindset should be embraced on a personal level as well.

In every interaction in life, there is something to be learned and explored. Everyone has a unique perspective that brings its own distinctive value. While we expect to learn from mentors, elders, or supervisors, I would argue we should aim to learn from all of our encounters.

As a personal example, each time I see my wonderful nieces and nephews (aged between four and ten as of writing this book), I leave with a new perspective and appreciation for something I had not considered previously. Children have a wonderful sense of curiosity, excitement, and raw emotion that gets dulled as they age. Regardless of their age, they teach me as much as I teach them.

The growth mindset can even be used in the way we eat, drink, consume entertainment, and interact with our communities.

Let's use food as an example. We're all guilty of having our "go-to" order when eating particular cuisines or at specific restaurants. Go ahead, think about your favorite restaurant—do you even need to look at the menu?

I'd bet you have a set of one to three dishes you choose from every single time. And while I understand the beauty of having this comfort food (I'm personally thinking of chicken-fried chicken at Cracker Barrel), I bet there is a plethora of other foods you would enjoy from that particular restaurant.

As I've embraced the growth mindset in my own life, I challenge myself to try new foods regularly. Yes, even at restaurants I dine at frequently. I still get my soul-warming comfort dishes from time to time, but if I do, I also try to order an appetizer, side, or even a whole second entrée I've never tried before just to experience something new. Hello, leftovers!

I won't lie, this has led to me trying some seriously disgusting foods (I'm looking at you, golden berries), but it has also led to me discovering some truly remarkable and delightful dishes with uniquely delectable flavors and textures. [37]

Don't get me wrong, those comfort foods still have a special place in my heart, but because of my growth mindset in this instance, other delicious alternatives have also joined their ranks.

As you consider how to embrace the growth mindset in your own life both professionally and personally, let's learn a bit from the great John Wooden, one of the most accomplished coaches in basketball history, who said, "Success is peace of mind, which is a direct result of self-satisfaction in knowing you made the effort to do your best to become the best you are capable of becoming" (Wooden, 2021).

I believe this quote is encouraging us to embrace the growth mindset on our journey to self-actualization. And as you may recall from Chapter Four, self-actualization is the idea of being the best version of yourself.

Per usual, Coach Wooden said it best.

KEY CHAPTER TAKEAWAYS

- The growth mindset is all about believing we have the ability to learn and improve over time. With the growth mindset, our intelligence (along with many of our other

---

37 Golden berries were absolutely terrible in my opinion. It was like a tart orange, a sweet blueberry, and a grape tomato all came together to create a diabolical concoction of all of their features. Sometimes tastes complement each other, but in this case, it was as symphony of nastiness.

traits) is not something we are simply born with, but in fact, it is something we can cultivate and develop.

- Mistakes and failures are simply opportunities for us to learn and better ourselves for the future.
- As with most things in life, our passions take time, effort, and dedication to cultivate. When times get tough, those with the growth mindset are more likely to work toward a solution and not simply give up, saying, "It wasn't meant to be."
- Science has disproven the old expression, "You can't teach an old dog new tricks." Our brains do, in fact, maintain the ability to learn, grow, and improve, regardless of age.

GROWTH MINDSET IN PRACTICE

Exercise 1: Every day, ask yourself:

- What did I learn today?
- Did I attempt something new today?
- Did I actively listen to others to better understand their points of view?
- Did I make a mistake and try to learn from it?

Exercise 2: Ask for honest feedback from the people in your life. This can be in the professional setting, but I also encourage you to consider trying this with your partner, close friends, parents, and siblings on a personal level. Choose three people in your life you interact with regularly and set up time for reflection. During the reflection, ask:

- How am I performing (as a coworker, as a daughter, as a son, as a partner, as a friend, etc.)? *This can be a simple*

open-ended question or you can ask for a rating (1–10)
with rationale.

- What do I do well?
- What can I improve upon?
- If someone came to you and asked, "What is my super-power", what would you say?

Note on Receiving Feedback: Though hearing negative or constructive feedback can be difficult, receiving feedback is vital to learning and growing as individuals. Feedback is extremely valuable and, unfortunately, very difficult to get regularly in life. And for some reason, we only think of feedback in the work setting, although it is immensely useful in all facets of life.

When receiving feedback, be sure to:

- Assume good intentions—after all, this is a close contact of yours.
- Actively listen and ask follow-up questions as needed.
- As hard as it may seem, regardless of whether you are receiving a compliment or constructive feedback, do not immediately react, deflect, or become defensive.
- Thank the individual for the feedback. Giving meaningful feedback can also be a difficult and awkward exercise for the person providing it.
- Reflect on the feedback you received.
- Create tangible, specific, and timebound steps to make progress around the areas for improvement.
- Set a follow-up meeting (quarterly, biannually, yearly, etc.) to repeat the exercise and track progress.

CHAPTER 10 WORKBOOK
TIME TO TRY IT!

GROWTH MINDSET IN PRACTICE

Instructions: As you work to integrate the growth mindset into your daily routine, let's build a plan to actively incorporate learning and development into your next week.

What did you learn today?

What is something you will work to learn more about in the next week?

Did you attempt something new today? If yes, what was it? If no, can you identify ways to increase the likelihood you will try something new tomorrow?

Name something new you will try in the next week. How will you ensure you follow through?

Did you actively listen to someone to better understand their point of view? What did you notice during this interaction?

How will you ensure you improve your actively listening skills moving forward?

What mistake did you make recently? What lessons did you learn from this mistake? What can you do to avoid the same mistake in the future?

RECEIVING FEEDBACK IN PRACTICE

Instructions: Identify three people in your life you will ask for feedback from. Reach out to these individuals today and let them know you would like to receive honest feedback from them. Determine how you will receive the feedback (i.e., in person, phone, videocall, e-mail, etc.) List the three individuals and the feedback format for each person below.

1.

2.

3.

Reminder – Questions you can pose during your feedback session include things like:

- How am I performing (as a coworker, as a daughter, as a son, as a partner, as a friend, etc.)? *This can be a simple, open-ended question or you can ask for a rating (1–10) with rationale.*
- What do I do well?
- What can I improve upon?
- If someone came to you and asked, "What is my superpower," what would you say?

Reflection & Results: How did each conversation go? What did you learn about yourself? What did you learn about your relationship with this person?

1)

2)

3)

Challenge! After your three feedback conversations, identify three areas you can improve upon in the upcoming month based upon the feedback you received.

Areas for Improvement:

1)

2)

3)

Action Plan: Create an action plan on how you can take tangible steps in the next month to improve upon the areas you listed above:

1)

2)

3)

Follow-up: Schedule follow-up calls for one month from today with those individuals who provided feedback to you regarding the three areas of improvement you listed above. These calls will act as accountability. How have you improved over the past month in the eyes of those who provided you feedback?

1)

2)

3)

CHAPTER 11

Be like a Scientist and Run Some Experiments

———

Tactics to Consider in Your Journey to Redefining Success

I love data. Go ahead, call me a nerd. I've enjoyed numbers and science since I was a kid, but all of my years working in the healthcare industry have just made my love for data and experimentation grow over time.

I've now had the privilege of working in cancer research, clinical diagnostics, neuroscience, and cardiovascular disease. While all of these areas pose their own unique set of problems, neuroscience really racked my brain. (Ha! See what I did there?)

Because of my work in Alzheimer's, Parkinson's, the opioid crisis, and major depressive disorder, I have a newfound appreciation for the power of the human brain. Our brains have the ability to make us feel better, experience side effects, or even perceive pain differently—even if nothing has changed other than our beliefs!

You see, one problem we suffer from in clinical trials, particularly in neuroscience, is the placebo effect. If you're unfamiliar, a placebo is a fake treatment (sugar pill, saline injection, etc.) that looks exactly like the medicine being tested.

In certain clinical trials, patients will be randomly assigned to either receive the real treatment or a placebo. The placebo effect is when the patients who are given the placebo treatment, something that should literally change nothing, experience a response due to this fake treatment. How can this be?

Because our brains are unbelievable!

To put some numbers behind how profound the placebo effect can be, clinical trials for antidepressants have an average placebo response rate of 36 percent, with some trials reporting up to a 70 percent placebo response rate (Meister et al., 2020)!

In clinical trials for pain management (opioid and non-opioid treatments), scientists have found placebo effects and patient expectations account for up to 50 percent of the effectiveness of pain treatments (Colloca, 2019).

As you can imagine, when placebo response rates are this high, it is nearly impossible for a company to prove their treatment is actually doing anything. After all, if a simple sugar pill is having such a large effect, the medicine better be pretty incredible.[38]

Because of this, there are tragically high failure rates in the clinical trials for these types of diseases. Okay, great, so now that we've established neuroscience clinical trials are hard, you may be asking, "Why on earth are you sharing all of this?"

Because this realization that the brain can outperform sophisticated medicines and science made me open my eyes to the power that simple brain exercises, mindsets, and beliefs can have on our wellbeing. We've already learned about the benefits of vulnerability, the growth mindset, and gratitude in our quest to Redefine Success, but I'm happy to share that there is a wealth of other tactics available to us as we work to reflect, prioritize, and realign our lives to achieve greater happiness and fulfillment.

To be clear, this is not an exhaustive list of tactics nor a one size fits all situation. These are simply the tactics that were most prevalent in my interviews and research. I acknowledge that not all of these tactics will likely work for you. Hell, if you're like me, you might even think some of the tactics sound like pie in the sky mumbo-jumbo before you try them.

But I implore you to keep an open mind and play the part of the scientist: experiment with each tactic listed at least

---

38 Some of the high placebo effect rates that have been reported may have been due to poor clinical trial design. Scientists continue to research and test different trial designs in hopes of taming the placebo effect.

once to see if you like it or not. Sounds a lot like the growth mindset, doesn't it? In actuality, I recommend you try each tactic daily for no less than two weeks to get into a groove and feel some effects. As with any good experiment, I bet you'll be surprised by the results!

MINDFULNESS & MEDITATION

I won't lie; prior to going on this personal development journey of mine, I naively thought mindfulness and meditation were things reserved for Buddhist monks, spiritual leaders, and hippies. Things like sitting quietly, focusing on my breathing, and repeating a mantra sounded like a big waste of time. But like I said, I was very naïve and admittedly wrong.

SO WHAT'S THE DIFFERENCE BETWEEN MINDFULNESS AND MEDITATION ANYWAY?

While both mindfulness and meditation are important and interconnected, mindfulness and meditation are in fact distinct from one another. The primary difference is mindfulness keeps your attention on yourself while meditation aims to take the attention off of yourself. More specifically, mindfulness aims to increase awareness of your emotional state, the present moment, and mental processes. Meanwhile, meditation aims to increase your personal awareness by focusing on an object of attention, oftentimes a mantra.

MEDITATION IS NEARLY AS OLD AS DIRT!

In my journey to learn about mindfulness and meditation, I was fortunate to have been taught by Bertrand Bouhour, adjunct professor at Georgetown University, and Laurence

Freeman, a Benedictine monk. Laurence shocked me when he shared the history of mindfulness and meditation throughout human history.

Meditation as we currently know and define it has been around for approximately thirty-five hundred years. But the practice of finding peace through silence, pursuing profound attentiveness, and searching for deep consciousness can be traced back to aboriginal cultures in Australia nearly forty thousand years ago! During this time, members of society emphasized the power of listening, patience, and awareness through what they called "dadirri."

Moving forward to around 1500 BCE, meditation can be found more concretely throughout a plethora of cultures. What's baffling is that despite limited means of communication, differing cultures, and vast distances, meditation is present in nearly every major religion, including Hinduism, Buddhism, Judaism, Christianity, and Islam.

Regardless of your religious beliefs, it's clear the ability to calm one's mind, become more attentive, and be more present through mindfulness and meditation has great value given the importance so many religions and cultures have put on the practice.

THE BENEFITS OF MINDFULNESS & MEDITATION—SCIENTIFIC FINDINGS

The US Agency for Healthcare Research and Quality has published research supporting mindfulness as a means to reduce anxiety, pain severity, and depression. Additionally, there are studies that point to mindfulness as a means to lower blood pressure, reduce cortisol levels, and change gene expression (Horton, 2014).

What's even more astonishing is that by using neuroimaging, researchers found the practice of mindfulness actually changes brain function and structure in a variety of regions. That's right, by practicing mindfulness, you can actually change the way your brain looks and acts![39]

In fact, mindfulness and meditation are so powerful that they are also being used as treatments for a myriad of conditions, such as bipolar disorder, social anxiety disorder, chronic stress, and ADHD (Marchand, 2014).

MINDFULNESS & MEDITATION IN PRACTICE

My introduction to mindfulness and meditation came through an elective in my MBA coursework.

In my first year, I vividly remember seeing the class "Meditation & Leadership" listed as an elective. As I read this class title, I literally laughed out loud, turned to one of my peers, and said, "How the hell is that an elective for business school? What a joke!"

39　One specific benefit of meditation is it helps to break key connections between what Dr. Rebecca Gladding labels the "Me Center," or medial prefrontal cortex, and the bodily sensation/fear centers, or the insula and amygdala. Additionally, meditation has been shown to strengthen the connection between the "Assessment Center," or lateral prefrontal cortex, and the bodily sensation/fear centers. In combination, these changes lower anxiety and allow for more rational thinking when presented with potentially dangerous or upsetting situations, leading to not only less anxiety, but also better outcomes (Gladding, 2013).

While I didn't take the class in my first year, I heard rave reviews from my peers who took the class about how it radically changed their thinking. So naturally, I was intrigued and had to try it. Also, I figured it would be an easy A![40]

Now in hindsight, I must admit the class was transformational. As with most classes, the quality of the class must be credited to my professors, led by Bertrand Bouhour.

Bertrand has a remarkable story of his own. Born and raised in France, Bertrand spent the first twenty-five years of his career developing and growing a performance management software company which eventually became so large it was publicly traded. Having met many people from the highly competitive world of tech, I can tell you this is no easy feat.

So naturally, after spending all of this time developing this impressive business, Bertrand decided his next step in life would be to become…a baker.

That's right. Bertrand transitioned from high-powered tech executive to bread maker. No, I don't mean making money, I mean literally baking bread. He also happened to land a teaching gig at Georgetown University as an adjunct professor.

In hearing his story in class and interviewing him for this book, it's abundantly clear that every decision Bertrand has made in life revolved around two things: "For me, what really matters, first of all, is the people in my life. The second thing

---

40 Funny enough, I only got an A- in the class. So much for an easy A!

is my own self-discovery and personal journey toward better understanding who I am."

When asked where his mindset, appreciation for life, and deep understanding of his personal priorities stem from, he first credits attending a five-day silent retreat filled with meditation at the age of eighteen. Can you imagine not saying a single word for five days?

Well, apparently, these five days were life-altering. "It really changed my life because I had a kind of revelation. Not in a very mystical way...but in a way I started to have great interest in understanding aspects of life much better. What was the meaning of life? What was love? How should I have a good life? And so on and so on. It motivated me to define myself much better. So, I think that was the first event that really made me think differently."

Since then, meditation has been an essential part of Bertrand's life as he meditates a minimum of twice a day for twenty minutes a session. "The practice of meditation is a very, very important discipline for self-discovery and defining who you are as a person."

As a result of Bertrand's class, mindfulness and meditation have become a regular part of my life as well. Just like how I notice when I skip a workout, I can feel a difference in my thinking, listening, and emotions when I neglect to meditate.

My meditation practice has led to a greater ability to reflect and clarify my inner thoughts and priorities in life. That inner voice or gut feeling we heard about from many of our friends in Part One, like Bill Novelli, Terry McDougall, Patrick McGinnis, and Marissa Fernandez, becomes clearer with meditation.

Additionally, I am able to be more attentive and focused when speaking with others because I can notice when my mind wanders. It really is crazy how "noisy" and distracted my brain is, but meditation has helped me calm it greatly.

TIME TO TRY IT FOR YOURSELF!

Note—I've outlined some supremely basic instructions of how to meditate. There are a plethora of apps, online resources, and books that are entirely dedicated to mindfulness and meditation if this is something you want to learn more about.

- Sit down.
    - Find a place to sit that is calm and quiet. Sit up straight, plant your feet on the floor, and place your hands in your lap in a position that feels comfortable. As Laurence Freeman told me, "Avoid couch slouch." This should be a comfortable position you can maintain for the duration of your session.
- Take three deep breaths.
    - Really focus your attention on your breathing. Feel your chest expand and compress. Feel your body begin to relax.
- Set a timer.
    - Many resources will recommend twenty minutes, but admittedly, that can feel very long if you haven't been meditating for quite some time. I recommend you start with five- or ten-minute intervals.

- Close your eyes and feel your breath.
  - Feel the sensation of your breath as you calmly breathe in and out.
- Try to clear your mind of thoughts—repeat a mantra in your brain slowly and steadily.[41]
  - Inevitably, your mind will wander. That's okay! I don't know about you, but my mind is a noisy place. When you catch yourself thinking about something, just try to return your attention to your mantra and breath. Be kind to yourself and try not to judge your thoughts. There's no winning at meditation! But with time and practice, you will begin to notice the rewards of a regular meditation discipline.
- When your timer sounds, slowly open your eyes and return to your environment. How do you feel?

Again, if it's your first time meditating—or even if it's your hundredth time—you are likely to feel more relaxed and perhaps a bit sleepy after you open your eyes. You may also notice your brain is a "noisy" place that is constantly thinking and stressing about what you need to do next, how to handle a challenge, or what you may have forgotten.

---

41 The concept of a *mantra,* Sanskrit for "mind tool," began around 1000 BC. It's typically a simple word or verse that is repeated or chanted. The idea of using a mantra is by focusing your attention on the repeated word, you are better able to take your attention and thoughts off of yourself to achieve higher consciousness.

One of the most well-known mantras is "Om." That being said, there is a wealth of highly utilized mantras to choose from, so feel free to do some research and find one that resonates with you. You can even make up your own personal mantra if you'd like! In our class, we used "Maranatha" (pronounced "Ma-Ra-Na-Tha"), as the four syllables could be timed with our breathing. "Ma-Ra" during the breath in, "Na-Tha" during the breath out.

This is all completely normal. I still struggle with my brain wandering during meditation, but if it makes you feel better, Bertrand and Laurence told me they do, too, even after decades of meditating.

As you continue to practice and incorporate meditation into your life, you will find you are more aware of when your mind wanders during a conversation, when you feel overwhelmed, or even when your emotions may be getting the better of your rational thoughts.

Maintaining our attention on something is a rare gift that is now becoming a lost art. Whether it's on your own thoughts and feelings or with others, meditation can help you improve your focus and attentiveness.

Regardless of whether mindfulness and meditation suit your fancy, our next tactic was used by many of my interviewees and turns out to be a powerful tool to reflect and organize our thoughts.

JOURNALING

Now I don't know about you, but as I embarked on this personal development journey, I was very unaware of what journaling even was. I imagined journaling was a lot like having a diary as a kid. I never personally kept a diary, but what I gathered from the stereotypes in movies was every entry started with "Dear Diary" and inevitably included some form of teenage drama—a crush, a date, some juicy gossip, a school nemesis, etc.

But, apparently, journaling is decidedly different than keeping a diary. While a diary aims to log daily events and be more retrospective of what happened in a day, journaling is a deeper reflection that can be a way of becoming more future thinking.

Journaling can be a means of having a safe place to write about your emotions, brainstorm new ideas, organize your thoughts surrounding complex problems, or simply reflect, clarify, or prioritize your ideas or values (Holloway, 2021).

In a 2020 interview, with Hal Elrod on the *Achieve Your Goals* podcast, Yanik Silver (the author of *The Cosmic Journal* and founder of Maverick1000 we met in Chapter Five) shared the following about journaling:

"It's one of the foundational habits that can make us more aware, more successful. To me, journaling is really getting deeper. So, there's scientific proof that journaling...creates more happiness because it forces us to create. [It can] start bringing awareness to so much in your life. I use it for ideas that keep percolating, building and growing. I use it for expressing myself through my art. I use it for keeping track of these things. I use it for gratitude. Journaling, to me, it gets better and better with practice. It's like meditation. You meditate one time [and] you're not going to be calm, centered, present every moment. Journaling is like that."

Naturally, as soon as Yanik talked about the peer-reviewed scientific research, I had to dig a little deeper. Apparently, journaling—more specifically, expressive writing—has been studied at length and the results are mind-blowing!

Research surrounding the benefits of expressive writing date back to Dr. James Pennebaker's pioneering experiment back in 1986. Dr. Pennebaker, a psychology professor at the University of Texas at Austin, performed his seminal experiment by first splitting college students into four groups, three test groups and one control group.

The three test groups were all asked to attempt expressive writing by writing about the "most traumatic or upsetting experiences of their entire lives" for fifteen to twenty minutes a day for four consecutive days. The control group was told to write for the same amount of time each day, but to write about superficial topics like their room or shoes.

All of the students were then tracked for six months following their writing exercise. Shockingly, the students in the three test groups who had to write about traumatic experiences had fewer trips to the health center, missed less class due to illness, and improved physical health as compared to the control group!

The expressive writing experiment has since been repeated dozens of times in different contexts ranging from healthy volunteers to HIV, rheumatoid arthritis, or even oncology patients. Many of the studies have concluded expressive writing can produce long-term benefits both psychologically and physiologically.

Psychologically, scientists have found individuals to have better working memory, improved mood, reduced depression, lower stress, and higher performance. Physiologically, scientists have found improvements in blood pressure, lung function, liver function, and lower cortisol (a stress hormone) levels (Baikie and Wilhelm, 2018).

To be fair, there were several studies that noted some individuals who attempted expressive writing experienced upsetting short-term feelings as the participants reflected on difficult times in their lives. But the positive long-term effects have been repeated time and time again.

One fascinating study based out of New Zealand even found expressive writing improved healing rates in healthy subjects. Participants were again split into two groups: the test group performed expressive writing while the control group simply wrote about daily events. Participants then had a piece of their arm biopsied—a fancy word for cutting out a small chunk of their arm. After eleven days, 76 percent of the group who performed expressive writing prior to the biopsy had already healed while only 42 percent of the control group had healed from the cut (Rodriguez, 2013).

None of this is to say that the next time you get a cut, you should just journal. Scientists are not advocating for journaling as a replacement for other medical treatments. However, by journaling and performing expressive writing, we can lower stress levels and improve our immune response.

For our purposes, the benefits of journaling I want to focus on are the improvements in our working memory, improved mood, reduced depression, clearer thoughts, lower stress, and higher performance. All of these outputs will prove to be immensely helpful in our journey to Redefine Success for ourselves.

In addition to expressive writing, there are other journaling techniques and writing prompts that aim to help with reflection, clarity, and prioritization. By journaling about your desires, ideas, aspirations, and life goals, you are forced to listen to your inner voice and organize your thoughts.

Taking a few minutes to answer prompts, like the ones below, that make you reflect can lead to impactful realizations for yourself.

- What is your greatest fear? Do you think it is realistic? Why or why not?
- Write your own obituary. How does this align with how you spend your time and energy?
- What does it mean to be a good friend? What type of friend are you?
- How would you describe yourself to someone who had never met you? Write your description as though you were a character in a book or movie.
- Who is your hero? What do you admire about him or her?
- What is the hardest truth you've ever learned?
- What is your greatest dream in life?

As with pretty much anything, you can find an almost endless list of journaling prompts online if you would like to find additional questions to ponder.

While mindfulness, meditation, and journaling are just a few tactics to consider, they are some of the most cited I came across in my own personal journey. That being said, if these don't work for you, it's time to put on your metaphorical lab coat and begin your own research on other tools to experiment with in your own journey to Redefine Success for yourself!

CHAPTER 11 WORKBOOK
TIME TO TRY IT!

MEDITATION IN PRACTICE

Instructions: Plan to meditate five times in the next week. Schedule the meditation into your calendar to build in accountability. Write down your scheduled date, time, and duration for each of the five meditation sessions below. Aim to meditate for at least five minutes during each session.

Session 1:

Session 2:

Session 3:

Session 4:

Session 5:

Reflection & Results: How did your meditation go? What did you notice about your mind and body during your meditation practice? How do you feel after meditating?

Session 1:

Session 2:

Session 3:

Session 4:

Session 5:

Challenge! Establish a daily meditation practice. Block off your schedule for the same time every day for a minimum of ten minutes (twenty minutes preferred). The goal is to meditate for the next thirty days.

Reflection & Results: After your thirty-day meditation practice, answer the following questions:

How did your meditation practice go?

How has daily meditation impacted your life?

How has your mind or body changed after your month-long meditation practice?

How has your ability to focus or listen changed over the last month?

How has your ability to stay calm in stressful situations changed over the last month?

How will you incorporate mindfulness and meditation into your life moving forward?

JOURNALING IN PRACTICE

Instructions: Choose your favorite journaling prompt from the list at the end of Chapter Eleven.

Write the Prompt Here:

Write Your Answer Below:

Challenge! Create a designated journal to establish a daily journaling routine for yourself. Block off your schedule for the same time every day for a minimum of five minutes (ten minutes preferred). Every day, pick a new journaling prompt and take a minimum of five minutes to reflect and answer the prompt for yourself. The goal is to journal every day for the next thirty days.

Reflection & Results: After your thirty-day journaling practice, answer the following questions:

How did your journaling practice go?

How has daily journaling impacted your life?

How will you incorporate journaling into your life moving forward?

CHAPTER 12

Redefining Success
in Action

**Reflection, Prioritization, and Realignment of
Your Life through Development of a Life Plan**

This is it, the moment you've been waiting for. It's time for
you to define what success means for yourself!

We've now heard from amazing individuals who went
through a powerful personal journey to Redefine Success
for themselves.

We dove into the research to learn that happiness comes
more from our mindsets than from our circumstances,
striving for the upper levels of Maslow's pyramid is crucial
to feeling fulfilled, and our priorities and North Star will
constantly change throughout our lives due to our own personal development, regular life "disruptors," and dreaded
"Oh Shit Moments."

We explored the importance of relationships and the toxicity of comparing ourselves to others. We learned about key mentalities and tactics to employ in our pursuit for living better aligned with our priorities to maximize our happiness and fulfillment, as well as powerful practices such as vulnerability, the growth mindset, gratitude, mindfulness and meditation, and journaling to name a few.

But if you're like me, you might be thinking, "Okay, great. But where do I even start? What on earth are my priorities and how the hell am I supposed to balance all of them?"

Have no fear, Chapter Twelve is here!

One exercise I found instrumental in my own journey was the creation of a Life Plan.

Creating a Life Plan was the final assignment given to me by Professor Jeff Reid for one of my MBA classes. This was simultaneously the easiest, hardest, and most impactful final I ever had to complete.

It was easy because there literally was no wrong answer. After all, it was all about my life, priorities, and aspirations. There was nothing to memorize or get wrong.

Yet, it was insanely difficult. Because to do it thoroughly and correctly meant figuring out what the hell my life would look like if I had my way. It's like writing a movie script with yourself as the main character!

After spending hours creating this Life Plan for myself, it was abundantly clear that my previous perceptions of what I wanted for my life were insanely misbalanced and impossible to achieve. With my previous definition of "success," there simply was not enough time in the day to accomplish everything I wanted in all of the facets of my life.

But after carefully thinking through my Life Plan, my goals and vision for the future became clearer than they had ever been. I better understood my priorities and how they all fit together.

This exercise was a game changer for me, and while I have taken some liberties to adjust the original framework for our purposes, I must give credit where credit is due, as the Life Plan Framework I will share with you is inspired by Jeff's final assignment.

So, thanks, Jeff! Jeff also credits his former professor, Dr. Gerald Bell from the University of North Carolina, Kenan-Flagler Business School, for previously introducing him to a version of the exercise.

The instructions seem easy when you read them, but if you take the time to think through each section, you will find that providing detailed and thorough answers is supremely challenging.

To give you a sense of length and detail, my Life Plan wound up being seven pages, single-spaced in a Word document. Feel free to make it as long or short as you like. As with the other chapters in Part Two, I have also provided some Workbook pages for you at the end of the chapter.

LIFE PLAN FRAMEWORK

Rationale:

While your circumstances and mentalities will change over time, articulating your priorities, goals, and plans can be a powerful motivator to realign your life and increase your happiness and fulfillment while you fulfill your aspirations. Importantly, this is not a static document, as your priorities will inevitably change as you progress through life. That being said, this exercise was immensely helpful in my own journey to define my priorities and achieve better alignment across the many facets of my life.

To Start:

- What legacy do you hope to leave when your life is over?

Once You Have Clearly Stated Your Desired Legacy:

- **For Each Category Listed Below, Answer the Following:**
    - How important is this topic to you? What are your key values related to this topic?
    - What are your short-term goals? What actions will you take toward achieving them?
    - What are your long-term goals? What actions will you take toward achieving them?
    - How often and/or at what milestones will you evaluate your progress and adjust as needed?
    - How does what you have written in this category relate to or impact every other category listed?

- **Categories to Write About:**
  - Career
  - Family
  - Finances
  - Fun
  - Health
  - Community & Religion
  - Self-Development

Be as specific as possible for each section and practice vulnerability, growth mindset, and gratitude as you reflect on your life to date and your vision for the future!

Guidance on Defining Values & Goals

As you think about your goals for each category, I encourage you to be as detailed and specific as possible. Thoughtful articulation of your values related to the major categories listed and your own life goals surrounding them will make it much clearer as to whether you have alignment in your life or if you're not on the right track given all of your aspirations.

However, by creating detailed goals and strategies, you will be much more prepared and likely to achieve everything you write down in your Life Plan. One option (not required) is to use SMART goals. SMART goals are Specific, Measurable, Achievable, Relevant, and Time-bound (Corporate Finance Institute, 2021).

LIFE PLAN IN ACTION

As I mentioned, the Life Plan you create for yourself is not the end all be all for what your life will become. But hopefully, it provides you with the ability to view your aspirations with a more holistic lens.

As you reflect on what you've written, take time to understand the time and energy commitment the activities and values you've outlined in each section will require. Is there enough time in the day, week, month, or year to allow you to accomplish your career, family, and fun goals when they are viewed in combination with one another? Do your aspirations for your career match your financial goals?

I originally had unrealistic expectations for my own personal goals and needed to rethink what truly mattered to me in life. After all, not everything can be a number-one priority. As an example, I realized it would be impossible for me to accelerate my career to become a C-suite executive *and* be home consistently to spend time with my family, have time for vacations, and enjoy the activities I listed in my "Fun" section.

So, I had to ask myself: what matters most?

I can tell you for me, it is family, but the beauty and horror of the Life Plan is there are no wrong answers and your answers can change over time. What you care about today may not be what you choose to prioritize next year. As we saw time and time again throughout Part One, our North Star can, and likely will, change over time.

So, as you think about your own Life Plan, I would encourage you to set reminders to revisit your plan on a regular basis. I can tell you I have set up time for my wife and I to review each other's Life Plan every six months. We literally have set calendar reminders for ourselves to ensure we perform this crucial reflection twice a year! This is a great opportunity for us to understand if our priorities have shifted and ensure that we are regularly discussing our individual and shared visions for our life together. This is also a time for us to have honest conversations of how to better align our lives around our priorities if needed.

In case this seems daunting due to time commitment requirements, we usually allocate one to two hours for our discussion every six months. Of course, we can always add more time or follow up if things have changed drastically, because in that case, we have a lot to discuss!

Questions you should ask yourself as you perform your periodic review are:

- Have my priorities changed since I last wrote my Life Plan?
  - If so, how have they changed? What are my priorities now?
  - If not, how am I doing? Am I living aligned with what I wrote out as my priorities?
- What tangible steps can I take to achieve better alignment in my life around the priorities and goals I've outlined?
- If applicable, how does my updated Life Plan align with my partner's?

While it may seem simple, the creation of my Life Plan has fundamentally improved my vision for my future. It was an incredible way for me to look at my life holistically and better understand how all of the moving pieces fit together. Otherwise, time moves so quickly it is easy to go through the motions and get lost along the way, leading to a life that is misaligned with our true priorities.

Revisiting my Life Plan every six months is a great reminder of what truly matters to me. Even if I must adjust my Life Plan because my priorities have shifted, the exercise of writing down my current priorities, values, and aspirations is a great way to redefine what success means to me.

CHAPTER 12 WORKBOOK
TIME TO TRY IT!

LIFE PLAN IN PRACTICE

Instructions: On each page, answer the questions posed. Be as specific as possible!

Legacy:

What legacy do you hope to leave when your life is over?

CAREER

How important is this topic to you? What are your key values related to this topic?

What are your short-term goals? What actions will you take toward achieving them?

What are your long-term goals? What actions will you take toward achieving them?

How often and/or at what milestones will you evaluate your progress and adjust as needed?

How does what you have written in this category relate to or impact every other category of your Life Plan?

FAMILY

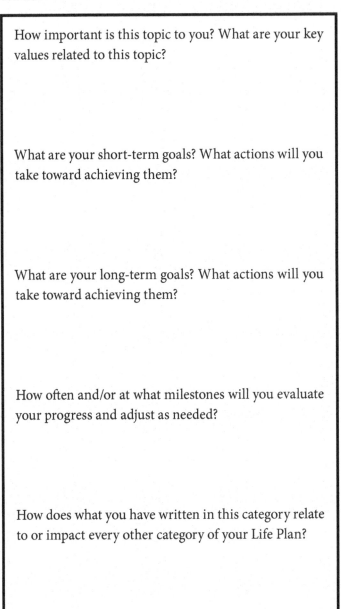

How important is this topic to you? What are your key values related to this topic?

What are your short-term goals? What actions will you take toward achieving them?

What are your long-term goals? What actions will you take toward achieving them?

How often and/or at what milestones will you evaluate your progress and adjust as needed?

How does what you have written in this category relate to or impact every other category of your Life Plan?

FINANCES

How important is this topic to you? What are your key values related to this topic?

What are your short-term goals? What actions will you take toward achieving them?

What are your long-term goals? What actions will you take toward achieving them?

How often and/or at what milestones will you evaluate your progress and adjust as needed?

How does what you have written in this category relate to or impact every other category of your Life Plan?

FUN

How important is this topic to you? What are your key values related to this topic?

What are your short-term goals? What actions will you take toward achieving them?

What are your long-term goals? What actions will you take toward achieving them?

How often and/or at what milestones will you evaluate your progress and adjust as needed?

How does what you have written in this category relate to or impact every other category of your Life Plan?

HEALTH

How important is this topic to you? What are your key values related to this topic?

What are your short-term goals? What actions will you take toward achieving them?

What are your long-term goals? What actions will you take toward achieving them?

How often and/or at what milestones will you evaluate your progress and adjust as needed?

How does what you have written in this category relate to or impact every other category of your Life Plan?

COMMUNITY & RELIGION

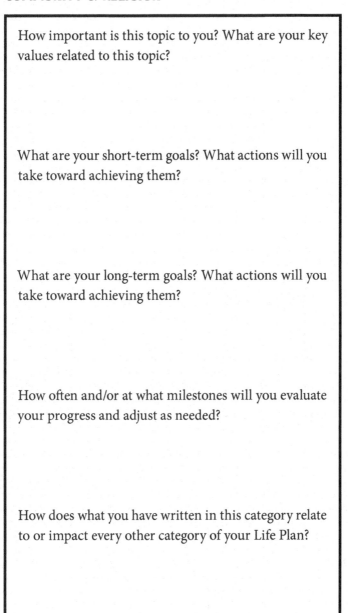

How important is this topic to you? What are your key values related to this topic?

What are your short-term goals? What actions will you take toward achieving them?

What are your long-term goals? What actions will you take toward achieving them?

How often and/or at what milestones will you evaluate your progress and adjust as needed?

How does what you have written in this category relate to or impact every other category of your Life Plan?

SELF-DEVELOPMENT

How important is this topic to you? What are your key values related to this topic?

What are your short-term goals? What actions will you take toward achieving them?

What are your long-term goals? What actions will you take toward achieving them?

How often and/or at what milestones will you evaluate your progress and adjust as needed?

How does what you have written in this category relate to or impact every other category of your Life Plan?

Challenge! Set a calendar reminder for yourself for six months from today to reread your Life Plan, reflect on how your last six months have gone, and adjust your Life Plan as needed.

Reflection & Results: During your six-month Life Plan review, answer the following questions:

Have your priorities changed since you wrote your Life Plan?

If so, how have they changed? What are your priorities now?

For the aspects that have not changed, how are you doing? Are you living aligned with what you wrote out as your priorities?

What tangible steps can you take to achieve better alignment in your life around the priorities and goals you've outlined?

Conclusion

Congratulations! You made it to the Conclusion. Which means either you:

- Read through my entire book and weren't completely scared off or bored. Hell, dare I say you might have enjoyed it? (Hooray for me!)
- Decided to skip to the Conclusion after reading the Introduction to learn more about my story. (Flattering for me.)
- Wanted to be efficient and cut to the chase about how to Redefine Success for yourself. (The joke is on you because that's mainly in Part Two. But I'll still take it as a win since you care about what I have to say.)
- You're a glutton for punishment and despite not enjoying the book, you made it to the end. (I'll take the victory nonetheless.)

No matter what option is true, you can see I consider you making it here to be a big victory, so thank you!

As promised, I'll now dive a bit more into my own personal story of Redefining Success and what led to me writing this labor of love. **Warning**: The next few pages are a bit more of a downer as I share more about my "Oh Shit Moment" and practice vulnerability and gratitude (hey there, Part Two). That said, I'll wrap this puppy up with more of my typical upbeat tone, so please bear with me.

MY "OH SHIT MOMENT"

It was June 2, 2016. I was suffering through my hour-long commute from Rockville, MD, to my home in Arlington, VA. As I sat in traffic, trying to drown out the road rage with the sound of sweet tunes, I got a phone call from my dad.

My dad often called when he thought I was on my way home to see how my day went, chime in with his sage advice on how to tackle an issue at work, and just generally catch up. This was no ordinary phone call, though.

As I picked up the phone, I learned my father had experienced some concerning symptoms over the past few months and decided to see a doctor. That was my first red flag, because my father never saw doctors.

The doctor ran some tests, and apparently one test in particular came back with some concerning results. So naturally, with his distrust of medicine, my dad insisted on a repeat test. The repeat test not only confirmed the original results, but came back even more conclusive than the original test— prostate cancer.

It doesn't take a genius to know those two words suck. I, having worked in cancer research for three years with a bachelor's in biology and master's in biotechnology, just happened to have a bit more insight into just how much those two words could suck.

The next two years involved countless trips to Philadelphia to join my father for surgery, radiation therapy, chemotherapy, blood transfusions, clinical trial enrollment, and a whole host of nasty side effects. Eventually, my dad lost his battle at the young age of sixty-two, passing away from a sudden brain hemorrhage caused by his illness on June 28, 2018.

This two-year stretch was the most exhausting and difficult time of my life. The toll cancer can take on an individual and a family is devastating. Even the seemingly mundane aspects of life are forever changed.

Let's use dinner as an example. As my parents had immigrated from Spain, family dinners were extremely important in my house growing up; it's a Mediterranean thing. Without fail, every night, we would all sit down together and enjoy dinner—no TV, no cellphones, just my mom, dad, sister, and I sitting around a table, eating and talking.

Well, it was more like my dad was doing 90 percent of the talking. Anyone who was fortunate enough to have met my father would likely describe him as a lovable, personable chatterbox. He literally could talk to a wall if he had to! I kid you not, there were times when he wanted a talking partner so badly he would purposefully say something controversial he knew my sister would despise just to instigate a heated debate. He didn't even necessarily agree with what he would say; he would just say it to incite chaos. It was like entertainment to him.

You could call our family dinners many things, but dull was not one of them. My father made sure of it. But as soon as he passed away, dinners became quieter. We've done our best to fill his voice, but it becomes exhausting and difficult to constantly come up with new topics of discussion, interesting facts, and probing questions. We never had to fill that role growing up because he did. Frankly, I don't know how he did it!

So, to this day we often find ourselves turning on music in the background to help fill the void of his nonstop voice. Don't get me wrong, we still have lively discussion, but it's just not the same.

That is just one small example of how even something as small as dinner conversation changes drastically with the death of a loved one. Needless to say, almost every facet of my family dynamic has changed since he passed.

As all of these changes crystallized, I found myself slipping into a darker place in my head. Frankly, I'm not sure I could have survived without the love and support of my wife, mom, and sister. His two-year battle with cancer had been more emotionally and physically taxing on me than I could have imagined. I can't fathom how he must have felt.

But as I tried to re-assimilate myself to normal life, I found my previous life no longer had the same meaning. I could no longer call my dad during my seemingly empty and endless commutes home, my job no longer brought me joy or fulfillment, and every aspect of my life, outside of my family and dog, either made me angry or brought me to tears daily.

I had hit rock bottom and desperately needed a break to figure things out. Twenty-nine seems a bit early for a midlife crisis, but I can't come up with a better description for what I experienced at that time. And so, my affectionate phrase, "Oh Shit Moment," was born.

After months of reflection and thousands of dollars spent on grief therapy, I came to realize I had originally modeled my life after my father's. I began my career forming a technical foundation in science—he did the same in engineering. After about five years, I leveraged my abilities to jump to the business side of science—he did the same in his career, again in engineering. And my career goal was to join the C-suite of some swanky biotech/pharma company in the future—a path that would entail a ton of work and dedication with a sprinkle of luck. As you can probably guess from the pattern, my dad accomplished this feat in the engineering world and worked his ass off to do so. So much so that for about ten years, he was traveling to England every other week for business. Unquestionable career success, but at what cost?

So, after much deliberation and discussion with my wife, I decided it was time for change.

In reflecting, I cannot understate how important bandwidth and time are to be truly reflective and purposeful about your choices. I fully acknowledge that if I had kids or did not have the support of my wife, this journey I took would have looked and felt much different.

I tip my cap to all of you who are parents, because the time and energy required to raise a little human is no joke! I hope to have that experience one day, but I took advantage of having the extra bandwidth in this case.

So, I decided to quit my job. But instead of simply quitting my job and giving myself six to twelve months off, I decided to be "productive" by society's standards and pursue my fulltime MBA. Perhaps not the best reason to get an MBA, but since it was something I had been thinking about for a while, it seemed like a reasonable next step. I viewed this degree as a chance to constructively add value to my life, explore new avenues, meet people, open doors, and have the bandwidth to find my next passion.

School always came naturally to me, so I would be able to do it in a low-stress way if I didn't get too involved in extra-curricular activities. With this mindset, I'd be able to use the MBA as a chance to clear my head, learn about different industries, and explore what other opportunities were present in the world. Hello, growth mindset!

Admittedly, I felt lost as I again had no idea what I wanted to be when I grew up, but I knew I needed to reflect, figure out the aspects of life I really cared about, and come up with a game plan that provided better balance in my life. Sounds a lot like Redefining Success, right?

MY PATH TO REDEFINING SUCCESS

During the first six months of school, I did it my way. While I did well in my classes, I did not spend much time socializing, getting involved in extracurricular activities, or attending school events.

My goals were simple: explore different industries that sounded interesting while giving myself as much bandwidth as possible to regroup and Redefine Success for myself.

As I explored different industries, I found myself pulled in a plethora of different directions. At various stages of my MBA, I seriously considered pivoting to careers in the wine industry, sports management, venture capital, consulting, professional/life coaching, and even entrepreneurship. I was all over the place!

Honestly, all of these paths still sound appealing to me for various reasons. However, as I reflected on my goals in life with a more holistic lens, improving patient outcomes through my expertise at the intersection of science and business still sounded like the sweet spot for me.

I became more involved outside of the classroom as I felt more confident about the path I had picked. In particular, I began working in the career center as a peer advisor, which opened my eyes to the fact that my struggle to figure out what to do with my life was not unique.

Most of my classmates were experiencing doubts about what to do next, how to push back against the external pressures to pursue society's definition for success, and how to balance all of the various facets of their lives. I thought, "Perhaps there should be a book out there about Redefining Success to help in these instances?"

I also met many of the wonderful individuals I introduced to you in this book via business school. From having Patrick McGinnis (the creator of FOMO) as a guest speaker in class, to being introduced to David Perkins (Founder of High West Distillery) through a connection created from a class assignment, to being taught meditation and leadership by Bertrand Bouhour (tech mogul turned baker), to meeting Bill Novelli (former AARP CEO) through the Georgetown Business for Impact group.

And, of course, Jeff Reid, professor of entrepreneurship, introduced me to the concept of the Life Plan Framework and encouraged me to pursue the path that was most appropriate for me based on my priorities in life.

In the end, while life decided to hand me an "Oh Shit Moment" in my late twenties that really sent me into a dark and depressing spiral, I now feel grateful for the new path and mindset I have acquired because of it.

I really appreciate this "new me." A "new me" who prioritizes happiness, family, relationships, fulfillment, vulnerability, growth mindset, passion, and science—hey, that's a lot of this book!

WHAT'S NEXT?

While I certainly don't have it all figured out, I at least understand my priorities and am armed with newfound knowledge,
frameworks, and tactics to maximize happiness and fulfillment by living aligned with my priorities and ensuring that
they are at the heart of all of my decisions.

We cannot choose when an "Oh Shit Moment" strikes, but
we can choose how we respond to it and how to grow from it.

The MBA and this book were my response. Only you can
choose how you will eventually respond. Better yet, you can
choose to Redefine Success for yourself now to ensure you
are better able to handle that difficult time in your life.

Admittedly, this book started as a selfish endeavor, as I simply
wanted to learn about how to attain happiness and fulfillment in life for myself. It also happened to be a bucket list
item! But as I learned, spoke with others through my peer
advising and interviews, and continued my personal growth,
it was clear that I wanted to share my findings with as many
people as possible to encourage others to not wait for life to
"bonk you on the head" (to quote Yanik Silver), but to decide
to live more purposefully, meaningfully, and happily today.

As we learned throughout our journey together, success
should be an internal metric only *you* can define.

Don't get me wrong, the journey to Redefining Success is
hard. You will need to be vulnerable and honest about what
really matters to you, even if it doesn't necessarily align with
society's definition for success. As the stories in Part One

highlighted, your definition for success will change over time, so your work is never finished. But in the end, this is your life.

So, I implore you: be kind to yourself, appreciate what you have, and start living your life in better alignment with what truly matters to *you*. I promise, if you put in the work, the fruits of Redefining Success are sweet and the juice is most definitely worth the squeeze.

Acknowledgments

When I first began this journey, my family would have said I was the least likely person to write a book. They say the best writers are avid readers, and amongst my family, I read the least by far. Needless to say, my family was not wrong. And yet, here we are...

But the fact of the matter is I cannot take credit for this book. While I may have written the words in my own tone and style, in actuality, this book is the product of hundreds of inspiring individuals! It was only possible due to the generosity of my interviewees, the tireless dedication of hundreds of scientists and researchers, and the overwhelming support I received from my own personal network.

First and foremost, I must thank my family. Without your love and support, I would not be the person I am today. Through your love and support, you all give me strength, courage, and inspiration. I cannot thank you enough. Mom, Dad, Steph, Marta, Jordy, Sydney, Lorraine, Tony, Mimi, Angie, Jeremy, Austin, Ranger, Allie, Jon, Zimmie, Mojo, Eddie, and Murphy—you all mean so much to me. I love you all!

I would be remiss if I didn't include a special thank-you to my dad, Ramon Biarnes. I miss you so much every day. You were taken from us too soon. But as a result of my grief after you passed, I underwent a transformational journey that led to writing this book.

A huge thank-you to Eric Koester, my author coaches, all of my fellow authors at the Creator Institute, and the fantastic team at New Degree Press. The book writing program you have created is truly incredible. Prior to finding the Creator Institute, writing a book felt like a nebulous process that seemed impossible to achieve. Thank you for demystifying the process and providing support every step of the way.

This book would not have been possible without all of the hard work and dedication from my *amazing* team of editors. In particular, despite never physically meeting either of you, Scott Aronowitz and John Chancey, I feel like I've known you forever. Thank you for your incredible perspectives and patience as you worked with me tirelessly to make my book a reality.

Just when I thought my book was nearly finished, I sent my complete manuscript to my beloved beta readers, Anisa Sanghrajka, Catherine Torlucci, Marta Biarnes, Ricardo Rendon Cepeda, and Steph Maniglia, who mercilessly and lovingly tore my book to shreds. Honestly, I think you all provided more feedback than my editors. Thank you, thank you, thank you for your invaluable feedback to take my book to the next level!

This book is only as good as the stories within it, which are *fantastic* if I may say so myself! Thank you so much to all of my interviewees for being so gracious with your time and entrusting me with your stories. Your vulnerability is inspiring and your journeys will positively impact anyone who reads this book. In order of appearance, thank you, Matthew Berry, Mike O'Donnell, Terry McDougall, Patrick McGinnis, Bill Novelli, Marissa Fernandez, Yanik Silver, David Perkins, Jonny Weitz, Apolo Ohno, and Bertrand Bouhour.

And to all of my friends and family from all walks of life—this book would not have been possible without you! As part of this book publishing journey, I elected to move forward with a hybrid publisher in order to retain the rights to my book. This meant I would need to raise funds for the publishing process through a preorder campaign. I vividly remember warning my wife that outside of a few copies to my closest friends and family, we should be prepared to fund almost all of the publishing costs. One hundred fifty-one individual orders later and my publishing costs were basically *fully covered*. The outpouring of support I received throughout this process was truly moving. Thank you all!

Nic Acton
Chelsea & John Adler
Phil Agbeko
Raheel Ahmad
Tosin Akinyinka
Eric & Meagan Annino
Eline Appelmans
Susan Baker
James Barry
Matthew Bess
Puspanjali Bhatta

Marta Biarnes
Salvador Biarnes & Eugenia Xancho
Elisabet Biarnes & Oscar Garcia
Monica Biarnes & Roger Carbo
Samuel Boafo-Arko
Bertrand Bouhour
Carol Brotherton
Ernest Canals

Marian Canals

Ester Canals & Greg
  Gillard

Maria Canals

Rosa Canet-Aviles

Dhananjay Chhatre

Baldev Chopra

Colleen & Curt Cimino

Kelly Colon

Maryann Connors

Erin Connors

Gregory Cothran

Stephanie Cush

Catherine D'Ascoli

Max Davidow

Morgan Davis

M Dianne DeFuria

Evan Delahanty

Koundinya Desiraju

Sandeep Dhillon

Ryan & Elise Dolen

Ariele Donahue Fleming

Martin Doyle

Miguel Echenique

Tilmer Engebretson

Jay & Ash Esteves

Marissa Fernandez

Elaine & Dan Fisher

Barbara & Bill Fisher

Connor Floros

Helen Freitas

Mitanshi Garg

Nina Godles

Jaime Goldstein

Adriana Gonzalez

Dori Gonzalez

Akshay Grewal

Abhimanyu Gulia

Sol Han & Youngu Son

Michelle Hayes & Ally
  Kershner

Stanley He

Will Hendrick

Greg Hiban

Dennis Hibbs

Zach & Jamie Hirsch

HanhLinh HoTran

Silas Humphries

Richard Ireland

Katherine Jackstadt

Ana & Stephen Kalasky

Aneesha Kapuganti

Harley Keh

Daniel Kelly

Jay Kenny

Anne Kilby

Kevin Klock

Eric Koester

Christopher Koslo

Mark Kourt & Monica
  Morales

Lauren Krasnodembski

Bryce Kruman

Meiling Kry

Dytrea Langon
Lauren & John Larson
Trey Lauletta
Ben Lee
William Lyons
Renee MacKenzie
Prashant Malaviya
Sumit Malik
Salony Maniar
Melissa Maniglia
Elvira Maniglia & Jay
Panico
Lorraine & Anthony
Maniglia
Allie Maniglia & Jon
Adams
Stephanie Maniglia
Angie Maniglia-Turner &
Jeremy Turner
Christian Marotta
Philipp Maximov
Michael McDermott
Matthew McLaughlin &
Katie Blosser
Megan McShea
Emily Morgan
Matthew Multer
Amrutha Murthy
Junior Mwemba
Sonal Nagpal
Vicente Notario
Michael O'Donnell

Emily Oler
Jameson Ondrof
Sarah O'Neill King
David Perkins
Erin Perugini
Lee Pinkowitz
Lianne Pinto
Helena Piquer
David Posawatz
Kieran Quinlan
Javokhir Rakhmatullaev
Aishwarya Ranganathan
Jeff Reid
KC Reinard
Ricardo Rendon Cepeda
Brianna Robinson
Ryan Rogers
Carson Rolleri
Jay & Jana Roth
Anisa Sanghrajka
Dan Sasso
Vince Sasso
Stephen Schiltz & Claire
Marcus
Suranya & Topher Schott
Melissa & Lee Siegel
Aleksa Sienkiewicz
Christopher Smith
Montse Soronellas
Mariona Soronellas
Misi Soronellas
Mercer Soronellas

Gopika Spaenle

Maria Teresa Piquer

Jim Thompson

Jacques Tran

Jordan Tsao

Sydney Tsao

Lina Vesterqvist

Alexander Williams

Mindy Williams

Avi Yogen

Ran Zuo

Appendix

INTRODUCTION

Hankins, Scott, Mark Hoekstra, and Paige Marta Skiba. "The Ticket to Easy Street? The Financial Consequences of Winning the Lottery." *The Review of Economics and Statistics* 93, no. 3 (August 2011): 961–969. https://doi.org/10.1162/REST_a_00114.

Merriam-Webster. s.v. "success (*n.*)." Accessed August 30, 2021. https://www.merriam-webster.com/dictionary/success.

MTV. "MTV Cribs." Accessed August 27, 2021. https://www.mtv.com/shows/mtv-cribs.

CHAPTER 1 – WITHOUT HAPPINESS, WHAT'S THE POINT?

Alda, Alan, and Laurie Santos. "What Makes You Happy?" October 20, 2020. In *Clear+Vivid with Alan Alda*. Podcast, 42:00. https://podcasts.apple.com/us/podcast/what-makes-you-happy/id1400082430?i=1000496188348.

Berry, Matthew, and David Meltzer. "Matthew Berry: ESPN's Senior Fantasy Football Analyst | #ThePlaybook 343." December 2020. In *The Playbook*. Podcast, 27:00. https://open.spotify.com/episode/10mfg4wG4OVQKBtsxSBmvU.

Cherry, Kendra, and Rachel Goldman. "What Is Happiness?" Last updated October 26, 2020. https://www.verywellmind.com/what-is-happiness-4869755.

ESPN Press Room. "Matthew Berry: Senior Fantasy Sports Analyst." Accessed August 25, 2021. https://espnpressroom.com/us/bios/berry_matthew/.

Kringelbach, M. L., and K. C. Berridge. "The Neuroscience of Happiness and Pleasure." *Social research 77*, no. 2 (Summer 2010): 659–678. https://www.ncbi.nlm.nih.gov/pmc/articles/PMC3008658/.

Sports Management Degree Hub. "The Lucrative and Growing Fantasy Football Industry." Accessed August 25, 2021. https://www.sportsmanagementdegreehub.com/fantasy-football-industry/.

Willingham, AJ. "Fantasy Football Is a Billion-Dollar Pastime. COVID-19 Is Wreaking Havoc with It." *CNN*, last updated December 5, 2020. https://www.cnn.com/2020/12/05/us/fantasy-football-coronavirus-challenges-trnd/index.html.

Valuates Reports. "Fantasy Sports Market Size Is Expected to Reach USD 48.6 Billion by 2027 - Valuates Reports." *Cision PR Newswire*. October 12, 2020. https://www.prnewswire.com/news-releases/fantasy-sports-market-size-is-expected-to-reach-usd-48-6-billion-by-2027---valuates-reports-301150193.html.

CHAPTER 3 – GOAL ACHIEVEMENT, FOMO, AND THE DESIRE FOR MORE

Alda, Alan, and Laurie Santos. "What Makes You Happy?" October 20, 2020. In *Clear+Vivid with Alan Alda*. Podcast, 42:00. https://podcasts.apple.com/us/podcast/what-makes-you-happy/id1400082430?i=1000496188348.

Evans, Lisa. "Why Reaching Your Goals Won't Make You Happier." *Fast Company*, March 20, 2019. https://www.fastcompany.com/90318268/why-reaching-your-goals-wont-make-you-happier.

IMDb. "Office Space." Accessed August 27, 2021. https://www.imdb.com/title/tt0151804/.

Jebb, Andrew, Louis Tay, Ed Diener, and Shigehiro Oishi. "Happiness, Income Satiation, and Turning Points Around the World." *Nature Human Behavior* 2, (January 2018): 33–38. https://www.nature.com/articles/s41562-017-0277-0.epdf.

Lykken, David and Auke Tellegen. "Happiness Is a Stochastic Phemomenon." *Psychological Science* 7, issue 3 (1996)": 186–189. https://doi.org/10.1111/j.1467-9280.1996.tb00355.x

Lyubomirsky, S., K.M. Sheldon, and D. Schkade. "Pursuing Happiness: The Architecture of Sustainable Change." *Review of General Psychology* 9, no. 2 (2005): 111–131. https://doi.org/10.1037/1089-2680.9.2.111.

CHAPTER 4 — FROM CLIMBING LADDERS TO CLIMBING PYRAMIDS

Evans, Tom. "All We Could Be: How an Advertising Campaign Helped Remake the Army." National Museum United States Army. Accessed August 31, 2021. https://armyhistory.org/all-we-could-be-how-an-advertising-campaign-helped-remake-the-army/.

Gross, Rob. "Corporate Social Responsibility and Employee Engagement: Making the Connection." Commissioned by Bill Holland, President, Mandrake. Accessed September 25, 2021. https://www.charities.org/sites/default/files/corporate_responsibility_white_paper%20copy.pdf.

IMDb. "Mad Men." Accessed August 31, 2021. https://www.imdb.com/title/tt0804503/?ref_=ttpl_pl_tt.

Maslow, A. H. "A Theory of Human Motivation." *Psychological Review* 50, no. 4 (1943): 370–396. https://doi.org/10.1037/h0054346.

Morgan Stanley: Institute for Sustainable Investing. *Sustainable Reality: Analyzing Risk and Returns of Sustainable Funds*. 2019. https://www.morganstanley.com/content/dam/msdotcom/ideas/sustainable-investing-offers-financial-performance-lowered-risk/Sustainable_Reality_Analyzing_Risk_and_Returns_of_Sustainable_Funds.pdf.

Nielsen. "Global Consumers Are Willing to Put Their Money Where Their Heart Is When It Comes to Goods and Services from Companies Committed to Social Responsibility." June 17, 2014. https://www.nielsen.com/eu/en/press-releases/2014/global-consumers-are-willing-to-put-their-money-where-their-heart-is1/.

Porter Novelli. "About." Accessed August 31, 2021. https://www.porternovelli.com/about/.

Sullivan, Erin. "Self-actualization." *Encyclopedia Britannica*. September 11, 2019. https://www.britannica.com/science/self-actualization.

CHAPTER 5 – WAITING IS OVERRATED

Albert, Melissa. "Arianna Huffington." *Encyclopedia Britannica*, July 11, 2021. https://www.britannica.com/biography/Arianna-Huffington.

Elrod, Hal, and Yanik Silver. "309: Make Your Journaling Cosmic With Yanik Silver." February 12, 2020. In *Achieve Your Goals with Hal Elrod*. Podcast, 39:17. https://halelrod.com/yanik-silver/.

Grant, Adam. "When Work Takes Over Your Life." April 2018. In *WorkLife with Adam Grant*. Podcast, 37:38. https://www.ted.com/talks/worklife_with_adam_grant_when_work_takes_over_your_life?language=en#t-7639.

Gunderson, Garrett. "Businesses Who Ignore This Trend Will Be On Life Support In 4-7 Years, Says Entrepreneur." *Forbes*, October 29, 2015. https://www.forbes.com/sites/garrettgunderson/2015/10/29/businesses-who-ignore-this-trend-will-be-on-life-support-in-4-7-years-says-entrepreneur/?sh=856d23377797.

Maverick1000. "Home." Accessed September 1, 2021. https://maverick1000.com/.

Moss, Jennifer. "Burnout Is About Your Workplace, Not Your People." *Harvard Business Review,* December 11, 2019. https://hbr.org/2019/12/burnout-is-about-your-workplace-not-your-people.

Stanford Graduate School of Business. "Arianna Huffington: 'We Are Drowning in Data and Starved for Wisdom.'" April 13, 2016. Video, 54:54. https://www.youtube.com/watch?v=vXz-VXRL07B4.

Tardy, Jaime, and Yanik Silver. "Yanik Silver – A $400,000 Slap to the Head" 2013. In *Eventual Millionaire.* Podcast, 46:58. https://eventualmillionaire.com/yanik-silver-a-400000-slap-to-the-head/.

The Editors of Encyclopaedia Britannica. "Midas." *Encyclopedia Britannica,* May 6, 2021. https://www.britannica.com/topic/Midas-Greek-mythology.

Thrive Global. "Home." Accessed September 1, 2021. https://thrive-global.com/.

CHAPTER 6 – THE NEVER-ENDING JOB

Arkes, H. R., and C. Blumer. "The Psychology of Sunk Cost." *Organizational Behavior and Human Decision Processes* 35, no. 1 (February 1985): 124–140. https://doi.org/10.1016/0749-5978(85)90049-4.

Kenton, Will and Khadija Khartit. "Golden Handcuffs." *Investopedia.* Accessed September 1, 2021. https://www.investopedia.com/terms/g/goldenhandcuffs.asp.

Kentucky Bourbon Trail. "About." Accessed September 1, 2021. https://kybourbontrail.com/about/.

Marsh, Calum. "The Rise of the Faux Bootleg Tee." *GQ*. March 17, 2021. https://www.gq.com/story/rise-of-the-faux-bootleg-tee.

Meet in Park City. "The History of Park City." March 28, 2017. https://www.visitparkcity.com/meetings/blog/post/the-history-of-park-city/.

U.S. Bureau of Labor Statistics. "Employee Tenure Summary." September 22, 2020. https://www.bls.gov/news.release/tenure.nro.htm.

Williams-Grut, Oscar. "Goldman Sachs Staff Complain of 'Inhumane' 100-Hour Weeks." *Yahoo Finance,* March 18, 2021. https://finance.yahoo.com/news/goldman-sachs-working-conditions-junior-analyst-presentation-inhuman-foster-care-hours-150437667.html.

World Population Review. "Utah Population 2021" Accessed September 1, 2021. https://worldpopulationreview.com/states/utah-population.

CHAPTER 7 – LIFE PIVOTS: THE NEW NORMAL

Bruce Feiler. "Life Is in the Transitions: Mastering Change at Any Age." Accessed September 2, 2021. https://www.brucefeiler.com/books-articles/life-is-in-the-transitions/.

Martin, Michel, and Bruce Feiler. "Author Bruce Feiler On Life-Altering Transitions." July 18, 2020. In *All Things Considered.* Produced by NPR. Podcast, 10:09. https://www.npr.

org/2020/07/18/892669586/author-bruce-feiler-on-life-altering-transitions.

Apolo Ohno. "About." Accessed September 2, 2021. https://apoloohno.com/about/.

CHAPTER 8 – VULNERABILITY: YOUR LEAST FAVORITE BEST FRIEND

Aron, Arthur, Edward Melinat, Elaine N. Aron, Robert Darrin Vallone, and Renee J. Bator. "The Experimental Generation of Interpersonal Closeness: A Procedure and Some Preliminary Findings." *Personality and Social Psychology Bulletin* 25, no. 4 (1997): 363–377. https://doi.org/10.1177/0146167297234003.

ASQ. "Five Whys and Five Hows." Accessed September 3, 2021. https://asq.org/quality-resources/five-whys.

Brown, Brené. "The Power of Vulnerability." Filmed June 2010 at TEDxHouston, Houston, TX. Video, 20:03. https://www.ted.com/talks/brene_brown_the_power_of_vulnerability?language=en.

Mayo Clinic. "Anxiety Disorders." Accessed September 3, 2021. https://www.mayoclinic.org/diseases-conditions/anxiety/symptoms-causes/syc-20350961.

Merriam-Webster. s.v. "vulnerable (*adj.*)." Accessed September 2, 2021. https://www.merriam-webster.com/dictionary/vulnerable.

Mineo, Liz. "Good Genes Are Nice, But Joy Is Better." *The Harvard Gazette,* April 11, 2017. https://news.harvard.edu/gazette/

story/2017/04/over-nearly-80-years-harvard-study-has-been-showing-how-to-live-a-healthy-and-happy-life/.

Simmons, Michael. "To Create a Real Connection, Show Vulner-ability." *Harvard Business Review,* May 9, 2014. https://hbr.org/2014/05/to-create-a-real-connection-show-vulnerability.

Toyota. "Why Is Your Company Called Toyota?" Accessed September 3, 2021. https://www.toyota.co.jp/en/kids/faq/f/01/02/.

Vohs, Kathleen D., Brian D. Glass, W. Todd Maddox, and Arthur B. Markman. "Ego Depletion Is Not Just Fatigue: Evidence From a Total Sleep Deprivation Experiment." *Social Psychological and Personality Science* 2, no. 2 (March 2011): 166–73. https://doi.org/10.1177/1948550610386123.

Wagner, Dylan, Myra Altman, Rebecca Boswell, William Kelley, Todd Heatherton. "Self-Regulatory Depletion Enhances Neural Responses to Rewards and Impairs Top-down Control." *Psychological Science* 24, no. 11 (2013): 2262–2271. https://doi:10.1177/0956797613492985.

Waldinger, Robert. "What Makes a Good Life? Lessons from the Longest Study on Happiness." Filmed November 2015 at TEDxBeaconStreet, Boston, MA. Video, 12:38. https://www.ted.com/talks/robert_waldinger_what_makes_a_good_life_lessons_from_the_longest_study_on_happiness?language=en.

CHAPTER 9 – GRATITUDE: THE ANTIDOTE TO TOXIC COMPARISONS

Alda, Alan, and Laurie Santos. "What Makes You Happy?" October 20, 2020. In *Clear+Vivid with Alan Alda*. Podcast, 42:00. https://podcasts.apple.com/us/podcast/what-makes-you-happy/id1400082430?i=1000496188348.

Christian, Bonnie. "UK Commuters Encouraged to Strike Up Conversation with Strangers for Happier Trips." *Evening Standard,* June 14, 2019. https://www.standard.co.uk/news/uk/uk-commuters-encouraged-to-strike-up-conversation-with-strangers-for-happier-trips-a4167766.html.

Dumas, John Lee, and Elayne Fluker. "How to Get Over the 'I Got It' Syndrome with Elayne Fluker." In *Entrepreneurs on Fire*. Podcast, 22:20. https://www.eofire.com/podcast/elaynefluker/.

Emmons, Robert. "Why Gratitude Is Good." *Greater Good Magazine,* November 16, 2020. https://greatergood.berkeley.edu/article/item/why_gratitude_is_good.

Epley, Nicholas, and Juliana Schroeder. "Mistakenly Seeking Solitude." *Journal of Experimental Psychology: General* 143, no. 5 (2014): 1980–1999. https://doi.org/10.1037/a0037323.

Geyser, Werner. "Instagram Influencer Sponsored Post Money Calculator." Influencer Marketing Hub. Last updated September 7, 2021. https://influencermarketinghub.com/instagram-money-calculator/.

Greater Good Magazine. "What is Gratitude." Accessed September 8, 2021. https://greatergood.berkeley.edu/topic/gratitude/ definition#why_practice.

Hunt, Melissa, Rachel Marx, Courney Lipson, and Jordyn Young. "No More FOMO: Limiting Social Media Decreases Loneliness and Depression." *Journal of Social and Clinical Psychology* 37, no. 10 (December 2018). https://doi.org/10.1521/ jscp.2018.37.10.751

Kingsley, Thomas. "Why the London Underground Is Called the Tube." *MyLondon,* June 16, 2020. https://www. mylondon.news/news/west-london-news/london-underground-called-tube-18429273.

Mir, Elina, Caroline Nova, and Meg Seymour. "Social Media and Adolescents' and Young Adults' Mental Health." National Center for Health Research. Accessed September 8, 2021. https:// www.center4research.org/social-media-affects-mental-health/.

Psychology Today. "Social Comparison Theory." Accessed September 8, 2021. https://www.psychologytoday.com/us/basics/ social-comparison-theory.

Solnick, Sara, and David Hemenway. "Is More Always Better? A Survey on Positional Concerns." *Journal of Economic Behavior and Organization* 37, (1998): 373–383. https://www.albany. edu/~gs149266/Solnick%20&%20Hemenway%20(1998)%20 -%20Positional%20concerns.pdf.

Summerville, Amy, and Neal J Roese. "Dare to Compare: Fact-Based versus Simulation-Based Comparison in Daily Life."

Journal of Experimental Social Psychology. 44, no. 3 (2008): 664–671. doi:10.1016/j.jesp.2007.04.002.

UC Davis Psychology. "Robert Emmons." Accessed September 8, 2021. https://psychology.ucdavis.edu/people/raemmons.

CHAPTER 10 – PASSION AND THE GROWTH MINDSET: TWO PEAS IN A POD

Dweck, Carol. *Mindset: The New Psychology of Success.* New York: Random House, 2006.

Elrod, Hal. *The Miracle Morning: The Not-So-Obvious Secret Guaranteed to Transform Your Life (Before 8AM).* Hal Elrod, 2012.

Fishbane, Mona. "Change is a Choice: Nurturing Neuroplasticity in Your Life." *Good Therapy* (blog). September 30, 2015. https://www.goodtherapy.org/blog/change-is-a-choice-nurturing-neuroplasticity-in-your-life-0930154.

Mindset Works. "Dr. Dweck's Research into Growth Mindset Changed Education Forever." Accessed September 8, 2021. https://www.mindsetworks.com/science/.

Moser, Jason, Hans Schroder, Carrie Heeter, Tim Moran, and Yu-Hao Lee. "Mind Your Errors: Evidence for a Neural Mechanism Linking Growth Mind-Set to Adaptive Posterror Adjustments." *Psychological Science* 22, no. 12 (October 2011): 1484–1489. https://doi.org/10.1177/0956797611419520.

Wooden, John. "America's Favorite Coach Wooden Quotes." John Wooden, Coach and Teacher. Accessed September 11, 2021. https://coachwooden.com/.

CHAPTER 11 – BE LIKE A SCIENTIST AND RUN SOME EXPERIMENTS

Baikie, Karen A., and Kay Wilhelm. "Emotional and Physical Health Benefits of Expressive Writing." *Advances in Psychiatric Treatment* 11, no. 5 (2005): 338–46. https://doi.org/10.1192/apt.11.5.338.

Colloca, Luana. "The Placebo Effect in pain Therapies." *Annual Review of Pharmacology and Toxicology* 59, (2019): 191–211. https://doi.org/10.1146/annurev-pharmtox-010818-021542.

Elrod, Hal, and Yanik Silver. "309: Make Your Journaling Cosmic With Yanik Silver." February 12, 2020. In *Achieve Your Goals with Hal Elrod.* Podcast, 39:17. https://halelrod.com/yanik-silver/.

Gladding, Rebecca. This Is Your Brain on Meditation: The Science Explaining Why You Should Meditate Every Day." *Psychology Today,* May 22, 2013. https://www.psychologytoday.com/us/blog/use-your-mind-change-your-brain/201305/is-your-brain-meditation.

Holloway, Sadie. "Diary vs. Journal: What's the Difference?" Felt Magnet. July 29, 2021. https://feltmagnet.com/drawing/Diary-vs-Journal-Whats-the-Difference-Between-a-Diary-and-a-Journal.

Horton, Richard. "Offline: Mindfulness – Evidence, Out of Place." *The Lancet* 383, (2014): 768. https://doi.org/10.1016/S0140-6736(14)60271-3.

Marchand, William. "Neural Mechanisms of Mindfulness and Meditation: Evidence from Neuroimaging Studies." *World Journal of Radiology* 6, no. 7 (July 2014): 471–479. http://dx.doi.org/10.4329/wjr.v6.i7.471.

Meister, Ramona, Mariam Abbas, Jochen Antel, Triinu Peters, Yiqi Pan, Ulrike Bingel, Yvonne Nestoriuc, and Johannes Hebebrand. "Placebo Response Rates and Potential Modifiers in Double-Blind Randomized Controlled Trials of Second and Newer Generation Antidepressants for Major Depressive Disorder in Children and Adolescents: A Systematic Review and Meta-Regression Analysis." *European Child & Adolescent Psychiatry* 29, (2020): 253–273. https://doi.org/10.1007/s00787-018-1244-7.

Pennebaker, James, and Sandra Beall. "Confronting a Traumatic Event: Toward an Understanding of Inhibition and Disease." *Journal of Abnormal Psychology* 95, no. 3 (1986): 274–281. https://doi.org/10.1037/0021-843X.95.3.274.

Rodriguez, Tori. "Writing Can Help Injuries Heal Faster." Scientific American. November 1, 2013. https://www.scientificamerican.com/article/writing-can-help-injuries-heal-faster/.

CHAPTER 12 – REDEFINING SUCCESS IN ACTION

Corporate Finance Institute. "SMART Goals." Accessed September 8, 2021. https://corporatefinanceinstitute.com/resources/knowledge/other/smart-goal/.